MANLY MATURITY

psychological approaches to personal development

P A McGavin

Publicious

AN IMPRINT OF PUBLICIOUS PTY LTD

Published by Publicious Pty Ltd
www.publicious.com.au

Legal Deposit Lodgment: (In accordance with the Copyright Act 1968)
National Library of Australia

Cataloguing-in-Publication Data
National Library of Australia
Author: McGavin, P.A. Dr
Title: Manly Maturity / Dr P.A. McGavin
ISBN: 978-0-9872221-4-5

Cover design by Publicious
Front cover photograph © under license from GettyImages
www.gettyimages.com.au

CONTENTS

Dedicated to the memory of my parents:

Basil John James Fry McGavin
Dorothy Isobel McGavin (nee Williams)

About this Book

This book is written mainly for guys. Some of it may "click" for our sister readers, and some of it may interest "gals" who want to learn more about "guys". Using the title *Manly Maturity* may imply that the main interest is boys and young men who want to mature as "men". But this is not quite the case. The prompt for writing this book arose from encountering a man near to my age who was wreaking havoc because he was very immature, and did not know how immature he was – and how *unmanly!*

That brings us to the *maturity* in the title. I love running as a sport and I love going to the gym, and this has enhanced my "manliness". I'll talk about the physicality of being a bloke in this book. But it's possible to *look* a great guy, but still just be a kid "inside". Mind you, I *like* kids, but when they are in the kid age group. No one likes an adult who's "just a kid". There's no particular virtue in being "old". But there is virtue in being "mature". A guy's maturity in physical terms may peak at say 30 years of age. A guy's maturity in whole-person terms may never peak. In this sense, the maturation process is on-going. That's why this book is not just about boys and young men. We all have eras in our lives: such as the era when we begin our first career job; the era when we start a family; the era when we consolidate family and professional lives; the era when we start surrendering professional life and start building different interests and activities.

In every era we build different activities. Retirement may be a big building time, because we may build neglected skills and start doing things that we've thought about for many years but not been able to pursue. But it's not essentially different if one is looking to age 20, or age 30, or age 40. In each life era there are shifts in our lives, and we consolidate different aptitudes and skills in these different eras. In brief, we *mature*. But this kind of maturing is not going to happen unless we *make it happen*. We are the chief actors in our lives. It is we who create the circumstances whereby we grow as persons – across a wide canvas such as our work lives, our family lives, our sports lives, our thinking lives, our life of prayer.

Now to the *psychological* in the sub-title. Understanding ourself as the one who enacts this making and taking of opportunities to engage with maturity, fulfilment, joy, and vigour in life's enterprise calls for certain psychological insights. In each era of living, we need to know how we think, how we process, how we respond to and create that complex unit that is "my life". This means psychological insight so that we direct our lives from within, rather than simply have them pressed upon from outside ourselves. As mentioned, this of course involves our physicality, but even more it involves our mind, our psych – our whole person. That's why *personal* maturation appears in the sub-title.

I've said a bit, but not said all that I need to say for you to assess whether you'd like this book. I am a religious man – a *very* religious man, a Catholic priest. Yet I've not written a "religious" book. That's why it's not in the title. Nor am I directly writing a "spiritual" book, because in a long life I have mostly found unsatisfying "spiritual" and/or "religious" books treating "growing". And that's not because I think spirituality and religion unimportant – quite the contrary. It's because they tend not to take sufficiently seriously the foundation of Christian and Catholic faith. That is, they don't take sufficiently seriously those foundational words from the first chapter of St John's Gospel, *The Word became flesh*. These key words do not simply mean "became *embodied*" by taking the form of a man. These key words mean taking the *whole of human nature*. It means, then, that I really can talk about "manly maturity" and speak about body + psych + spirit: that is, speak about the "whole man", the human *person*. So, although I adopt a psychological approach in this book, I have a keen sense of how this co-ordinates with what is spiritual and religious in Catholic terms. But the book can nevertheless be read by those who want to take away the psychological insights without necessarily taking up the wider integration of these insights as I see them.

I need to say a further word on the "manly" bit. People often do not realise how radical are the very ancient words, "And God made man, male and female he created them, in the image of God he created them" found in the opening chapter of the first book of the Bible. I cannot adopt any position that diminishes the dignity of women in the sense captured in this text. But the differentiation between human male and human female is profound. And there's only so much on can cover in one book, and so my focus is upon "guys". There's no "put down" of our sisters. If one does not respect girls and women, one cannot respect boys and men. It's just that I respect the differentiation between the sexes, and here treat *guys*. That's all.

I guess I'd better close this "About this Book" with a word about its style. It's not an academic book. It's not a racy read, but I've tried to make it friendly for anyone who is prepared to put in the time and to think through what I'm saying. I avoid jargon where it is unnecessary, and where it is needed I let the reader know the meaning of words that are not in everyday use. Often I adopt a conversational style, and so a "bloody" or two may be thrown in where it captures conversational expression of feeling. If a word such as "fuck" fits better than coitus, then I'll use it as a matter of expressiveness, not rudeness; if a word such as coitus better fits the context, then I'll use the latinism. I'm a scholar, but I've worked hard to try to write a book that's going to be read by ordinary guys who just would like some insights on being a mature man at whatever era of life.

P Anthony McGavin   **manlymaturity.com**
Canberra, Australia 2012

1

Psychology and Personality

Introduction

This book covers a wide canvas that ranges across discipline boundaries. The book needs mainly to be read from the wide perspective of "human development", rather than sub-discipline perspectives within Psychology and related disciplines.

The key word *Maturity* in the lead title is intended to appeal to human behaviour that is directed toward goals and outcomes projected into the future. This necessarily implies that conceived futures can have causal impact upon current behaviour that leads to changing future behaviours.

It is thus not surprising that the book should build upon an understanding of the human psyche that is not simply pre-determined, but that calls upon a dimension of self-influence that is both personal and social in the development of the human person. The sex and gender aspects of this developmental perspective focus upon males – as seen in the lead title, *Manly Maturity*. Following the sub-title of the book, this exploration is undertaken from the perspective of "psychological approaches to human development" and with a focus upon guys and the psychology and personality of guys.

"Psychology" and "Personality" can take varieties of meanings, and in order to introduce the topic, we first need some simple treatment of starting points for meanings as used in this book. Different meanings and different aproaches will unfold as the book unfolds. The different approaches here adopted will not have a generality for all readers, but the project undertaken in this book would become overwhelming unless certain self-limitations are adopted. I try to be "up front" about these.

We start of with "What is Psychology?" and "What is Personality?". The key point to which this first chapter moves is that personality profiles may be viewed in terms of a patterning of personality traits that form personality types, and that there is a range of personality types. In brief, although we are all distinct in our personalities, there are nevertheles sets of personality traits that outline our personality type. Understanding these personality types helps us to understand our own personality and other people's personalities. With this comes an appreciation of personality differences, and a readines to accommodate and to work with differing personalities. Nevertheles, personalities are not simply "fixed", and so appreciating the profiles of personalities provides a basis for approaching the development of personalities as is treated in the next chapter.

What is Psychology?

Most people will have their own idea about "What is psychology". The "logy" part of the term usually conveys a sense of "the *science* thereof", although that's not what it means in its original Greek root. The "psych" part conveys a sense of the *mind*, although in the original Greek root the meaning is nearer *anima* in Latin or *soul* in English. I mention this because there are different ways of thinking about the human person, and how we are constituted (for example, body, mind, soul, spirit). As a result there are different approaches to the human "psyche". It follows that there is not one Psychology, but a number of scientific approaches to understanding the human psyche. In this book I shall try to be transparent about what approach is used where. But such "footnotes data" as is necessary has been placed at the end of the book, and not in each chapter.

But it's not just different approaches to psychology that need to be noted. It's also different aspects of psychological questions that need to be noted. We probably tend to think of the psychology of a person as being "inside" the person, but social psychology will occupy us a good deal, and this treats our "psyche" in a social context and in social processes and interactions. Maybe we think of psychology as mainly about "thinking", but we will need to give a good deal of attention to "emotions" or to "feeling" as these are examined psychologically. So this just gives a bit of a preview of the scope of psychology. What I want to start out with is *personality*.

What is Personality?
Differing Personality Profiles

This again is a diverse area, and there is not one *psychology of personality*. I am first going to make recourse to one approach to the psychology of personality. The starting point for this approach is that we arrive in this world with the rudiments of a personality. This is a rather different starting point from one where the personality is viewed as mainly formed by the environment. I am not saying that the personality is not environmentally influenced. I'm only saying that I don't think that it's *simply* environmentally influenced, and that we arrive with the rudiments of a personality configuration. We see this, for example, in the way that some babies show themselves to be adventurous, while others show themselves to be timorous.

Having decided that this book is about guys (see "About this book"), it implies that personalities differ as between men and women. It's a long time back when a lecturer of the kind I thought would be strongly wedded to "socialisation" ideas, said in a staff room setting after the arrival of their third child and first girl, "We're not treating her diffently, she is treating us differently!" There of course is an awful lot of socialisation that goes into girl behaviour being different from boy behaviour. But I still accept the fact of difference between the behaviour of "guys" and "gals". That is, I think that we arrive with the rudiments of a personality, including sexual personality.

Just a note on my use of "gals". I'm just getting around the cumbersome business of saying "girls and women" as compared with "boys and men". So I just use "guys" for the older Australian idiom "blokes", and "gals" for the older Australian idiom "sheilas" – and hope that "guys" and "gals" will seem less "old-fashioned". Sometimes you'll notice I use both pronouns – his (her) – because there are contexts where sex or gender inclusiveness needs to be made explicit. An example of this is speaking about some aspects of the rudiments of personality profile that are best appreciated across guys *and* gals.

The basic categories for profiling of personalities are here presented as: extroversion/introversion; sensing/intuitive; thinking/feeling; and judging/perceiving preferences that one observes in different personalities. The examination that follows of this categorisation – even with simplicity and brevity – can be a bit tedious. Yet it is worth the attention in order to lay foundations for more dynamic appreciation of personality in the next chapter on Personality Development.

The acting preference of the personality: Extroversion/Introversion. The influence of socialisation of course is significant. A child may hide behind mummy's skirt because the child had some experiences that make for wariness. But we generally can pick the person who prefers a social setting where he (she) is centre-stage, or at least among the group that is loudest and most seen. And we generally can pick the person who tends to be more retiring, who has to be drawn out of himself (herself), and who prefers a smaller and less public social engagement. This of course is "in general". I am a rather introverted type, but I have little unease being up-front when I need to be up-front, although I still prefer quieter social situations.

When I was thinking about this writing I remembered something my Mother told me many years back. She said, "I remember when you were just in a cot, thinking to myself, 'That child has been sleeping a long time!' and so I went in to see. And there you were wide awake, and playing at making shapes with your fingers. You were like that always; you didn't seem to get bored, and amused yourself. You were no trouble as a baby." Mind you, I had my "trouble" episodes as I got older, because I had my own mind, and I required *explaining* – not *telling* – in order to adopt someone else's mind. But that's taking us forward somewhat, and I just tell this little story as an example of the rudiments of introversion in a very young child – that has persisted throughout life. The extrovert will be more looking for some sort of stimulating engagement to keep him (her) happy, and you can think of your own example!

The data-gathering preference of the personality: Sensing/Intuitive. Like most terms, the term "sensing" can have a number of meanings. On seeing this term you might imagine something like running your hand over a braile text so that you can work out the writing. Or you might think of the way your skin feels when it is buffeted by a salt breeze. What I mean however is more like a data-gathering exercise. How does one learn about the habits of Magpies: by watching them. Most people form their views about most things in this experiential or data-led way – that is, by *sensing*. If they havn't done the sensing exercise, they don't know about the "whatever". But this is not the way everyone prefers to proceed, and those who prefer intuition display different traits.

The intuitive person tends to get impatient with this step-by-step process, and looks for the "answer", or for the "proposition". This is because, those who have a preference for intuition like to grasp an idea first, and afterwards to reason it through. The intuitive person prefers to go straight to the point, and then to go through the reasoning process. Persons of this type may engage you to round-out their understanding or to check what is your understanding, especially if extroversion is also a preference. But intuitives have a different instinct from sensors in getting to understanding. Often it's because they are brighter in the cognitive sense. Conceptual aptitudes and skills often more call on intuitions. So someone who shows an aptitude for higher mathematics or prefers more cultured music listening typically is more intuitive, while someone who is good at going through complex processes that involve replication will usually have a stronger sensory preference in personality profile.

Of course, just as with extrovert/introvert, so also with sensing/intuitive preferences, one personality preference is not in and of itself better than the other. We need people with different personality profiles within any social setting. We are not all the same, and we can learn to complement one another. But achieving that complementing one another involves knowing and accepting both our own personality profiles and those of other people. And, as I shall later argue, this involves building upon these personality attributes. That is, although I think that we arrive with the rudiments of personality profiles, I do not think that is where it ends – and in the next chapter we shall explore *personality development*. For now, however, we turn to another broad personality attribute scale, thinking/feeling.

The data processing preference of the personality: Thinking/Feeling. Once again, we need to recognise that there is some restrictiveness in the use of these terms. If someone offends us, we're not likely to say, "I think hurt", but "I feel hurt." That's not the main sense in which I am using "feeling". We all know a social setting where someone has arrived and is trying to be a "nice guy" ("nice gal"), but who just isn't atune to what's going on with the group or with someone in the group, and is just goofing it! Such a person either doesn't have the sensibilities to gauge the social situation or isn't switched-on to gauge how others are acting and reacting. So it's the sense of the "social dynamics" that I mainly mean when refering to *feeling*. Some people seem to be just "natural" at this, and can with ease take the lead or fit in as suits the occasion, and their leadership style gains group assent or their social engagement just seems so easy. Others seem often to trip-up, and obviously just need more practice in these implicit social skills. It's not their forté. For some, "feeling" is not a strong natural aptitude in their personalities.

Such people are likely, by contrast, to prefer "thinking" as an attribute of personality profile. By this you might imagine something high-powered, like higher-level thinking; or you might imagine something private like thinking by oneself. I'm not mainly using the term in those senses. Extrovert people often do their thinking with others rather than alone, and often do it aloud rather than silently. We all know the type who relentlessly lets us know what he (she) is thinking, because there's this continuous monologue that usually wanders in a discursive manner. The "wandering" thinker or the thinker who often does not get far with his (her) thoughts may still be a *thinking* person.

Those who are more intelligent will usually think more quickly, and those who've had more education will usually think in more rigorous ways. But the person who prefers "thinking" will expect you to take him (her) through the steps to arrive at the conclusion, or will want to take you through the steps to arrive his (her) conclusion. The "feeling" person is not going to be so disposed to this way of processing – processing that we might call "cognitive" or "cerebral". The "feeling" person will be locating the processing activity in a social context and working it through in an inter-relational way. This "feeling" processing may, indeed, be "cognitive" in the sense that we shall deal with later when we examine *emotional intelligence*.

What we are dealing with is preference or emphasis on thinking or feeling that gives rise to a style of processing. The thinking personality tends to operate with the emphasis on careful reasoning, while the feeling personality tends to operate with the emphasis on situating what's being processed in inter-relational terms. The "thinker" is more cognitive, but not necessarily intellectual. Indeed, the "thinker" may not be very good at thinking and the thinking process may be clumsy and crude, but the "thinking" personality prefers to process in this manner.

The "feeler" may be cognitive, but not quite in the manner of the "thinker", and the processing is much more inter-relational or social. It also may not be very well processed. We've all experienced the person – more often a woman than a man – who is so busy dealing with how everyone "feels" or should "feel" in a situation, and where one of the kids just wants to say, "Mum, please 'cool it'! Just leave it alone will you; let it pass; now's not the time to go over this!" Now we come to the last attribute contrast in personality profile as I am here treating it; namely, judging/perceiving.

The personality preference for what-to-do- with data and data processing: Judging/ Perceiving. I'll treat the "perceiving" term first. This is in the sense of "looking at", "performing", "doing it". We all know what it's like to have someone who thinks that the purpose of a meal is just to "get it on the table", and it usually comes there with a "plonk". This is the person who doesn't really like cooking. Then there's the person who really likes cooking, and just *fusses!* Everyone else is ready to "cut corners", just to get the meal to the table, and get it done with. But the "perceiver" is caught-up in the process, rather than the conclusion of the process. It's the same when there's an argument, and one person just wants to go through it all again, instead of just leaving it, and moving on to the next thing – "Mum, just cool it; leave it alone will you!" Having spent my life as an academic, I think of the "absent-minded professor" as captured in comic strips, where the experiment is run and re-run, because the professor likes the experiment. I'm not like that, I will be patient for as long as it's needed, but I want to get to the conclusion!

The person who wants to get to the conclusion wants "closure", and in this attribute is a "judgement" type. We all know the kind of person who just won't hold back and look at the evidence. "Dad, if only you'd looked a the street directory before we set off, we would have been there ages ago! Now admit you made a mistake. Stop, and look at the map, and let's navigate more sensibly!" We all know when we've been just so grateful that there's been a "judger" around to cut all the unnecessary explorations and get to the point! But we also all know when someone has too strongly exercised his (her) preference for closure, and really creates problems because it's not so straightforward and a more careful judgement is needed, and revision of process and more evidence is needed before firming to a decision.

Yet again, all this is not "set in concrete", but the rudiments are there from the beginning. One child just likes putting things together, and it doesn't so much matter if someone trips over it; the putting together exercise can be done again. Another child wants the product not the process, and the finished result is what matters, and when achieved is to remain set. But this is before *personality development*, where personality traits get rounded out. And also this is looking at personality in isolation, whereas in real life different personalities complement one another, or at least may complement one another. For example, we need people who can undertake activity that has a high process content and where they can do this more or less happily. And we need people who can undertake activity that is high in decision-making content and where they can do this more or less happily. Sure, we all need to be able to do both process stuff and decison stuff, but we don't all need to do processing and decision stuff in equal proportions. The last phrase "in equal proportions" takes us to the next consideration in personality profiling.

One thing *or* another. I had a rather decisive, "J", Mother, who seemed often to say, "Make up your mind, son; you're doing one thing or another, not both!" In terms of the four scales here treated these preferences are:

extroverting (**E**) <u>or</u> introverting (**I**)

sensing (**S**) <u>or</u> intuiting (**N**) (the "N" is used because "I" has already been used)

thinking (**T**) <u>or</u> feeling (**F**), and

judging (**J**) <u>or</u> perceiving (**P**).

My Mother's demand in terms of the last scale, was "Stop perceiving, and make up your mind and *do* something!" That is, get out of your quandary! The point to note from this is that an integrated personality is "one thing or another". On the scales here proposed, **E** *or* **I**; and **S** *or* **N**; and **T** *or* **F**; and **J** *or* **P**. That is, in each of these dimensions, one is going to be one or the other – not simply in the middle (that is, at zero). One might be "near to the middle", and, for example, be only mildly **J**; or alternatively, mildly **P.** But in this approach for each of the personality traits, one will be one or the other, although in varying degrees – whether, say, "strongly **J**", or "somewhere-in-the-middle **J**", or "weakly **J**".

How do these different traits fit together.

The personality traits as so far considered need to thought of as having an interpretative shape. The last line (of **J** or **P**) is very important to the patterning of the interpretative shape of the personality. This is so because, if one is a **J**, then one goes straight back to the "processing" line – that is, the third or **T** or **F** line; and one's judgement will be expressed in either thinking terms (**T**), or in feeling terms (**F**) according to whether one prefers to process information in mainly cognitive terms or in mainly relational terms. So the last line matters a lot.

But the first line in this profiling of personality traits also matters a lot. Because if one is extrovert (**E**), then the world is going to know about it quite directly, and a lot of data will come out. If the data is of the sensory kind (**S**), that's what the world will hear; if the data is of an intuitive or concept kind (**N**), that's what the world will hear. Conversely, however, if one is introvert (**I**), then the world is not going to know so directly about the second line, about that data (be it of the **S** kind, or of the **N** kind), because the introvert doesn't so directly disclose. Instead, the world will learn how that data has been processed (the third line). So for an introvert with a **T** trait, you'll get cognitive-style or rational *reasons* for the conclusion (**J**); while an introvert with an **F** trait will also give reasons, but they'll be *relational* in nature and deal with how others think and feel about the conclusion. What you get "first up" may be modified with personality development, but it is "basic shape" that is here being presented, not "developed shape".

Now I can't here give you all the possible combinations of personality configuration, for there are many. But I need to give another example so that you get the idea. Take the last line in the configuration of personality traits given here, and change it to the perceiving trait (**P**). Persons with this trait preference do not go straight back to the processing line (the third line), but go straight back to the second or data-gathering line. And, if their preference is sensing (**S**), then they re-run the experiment and gather more sensory data; if their preference for gathering data is intuition (**N**), then they'll again try to give the data from the second line of personality traits a conceptual shape in order again to test for an answer.

The point, then, to note is that the configuration of personality traits fits together in a *structured way*, where the first and last lines of trait configuration have a key influence on the overall operational patterning of the traits configuration of the personality. Those readers who have some higher mathematics may perhaps see that the two preferences across four dichotomous lines of personality traits would generate sixteen configurations of these traits. That is, using this method, one can generate a matrix of 16 personality profiles. Well, this could get more complicated than I want in this book. The reason why I've drawn it to your attention is that I want the reader to be alert that there is quite a range of personality profiles. I can now speak to the implications of this.

Is there a pattern to the patterns of personality profiles? The answer is, *Yes*. Some personality profiles are rather rare. The data on this patterning may not be terribly reliable, and it may vary between cultures, but I'll just keep it simple and speak to the data to which I have access. My personality profile (introvert, intuitive, thinking, judging, INTJ) is somewhat rare, representing only about 3% of the male sample. The most common at 16% is the introvert, sensing, thinking, judging, ISTJ male – the guy who tends to be a bit quiet, who gives you sensory-data answers, and who gives this in ways that are cognitively reasoned, and who generally holds to the views that he gives.

The next most common at 11% is the extrovert, sensing, thinking, judging, ESTJ male – the guy who tends to talk rather more and louder, and is quick to give you cognitively reasoned answers, and whose answers are rich in sensory data, and who generally holds firmly to the views that he gives.

So you can see that over a quarter of guys have preferences that give a personality profile that we'd think of as "masculine" in our most common representation. That is, they are "men who know their mind", "men who give reasons", "men who like things to be factual", and mostly "men who are a bit quiet" – although there will be other men nearby who are like them in personality, but who are more up-front in their personalities and more forthcoming.

Now you might say, "Well, that's somewhat interesting, but I guess I already knew that." Well, "what we already know" often holds up under examination, but examination often reveals further things. To illustrate this, we'll look at the gals.

Is there a sex pattern to the patterns of personality profiles? The answer again is, *Yes*. At this point, one needs to be aware of the way that culture impinges upon all this. Imagine that you are in a culture where women are supposed to be quiet, and where girls grow up learning to be more demure: you are likely to get fewer extrovert (**E**) females under such cultural conditioning. And I used the word "sex" patterning, not "gender" patterning. "Sex" refers to whether you are male or female. "Gender" refers to whether such-and-such a behaviour is considered to be masculine or feminine – and what's masculine in one culture may be less-masculine in another culture. But more on that rather later. At this point, just accept that I'm refering to data that is sorted by sex. And my rather rare male personality type (INTJ) is even rarer among women, and less that 1 percent (0.8%) of the female sample. And the most common male personality profile, ISTJ, as a proportion of women is less than half of what it is as a proportion of men (16% for men, and 7% for women). And for the next most common male personality profile, ESTJ, the proportion of women is only about half of what it is as a proportion of men (11% for men, and 6% for women).

For the gals, the most common personality type is introvert, sensing, feeling, judging, ISFJ at 19%. That is, for about a fifth of women their preference profile gives traits of being somewhat quiet, being drawn to sensory data, being drawn to processing in a relational manner, and showing a readiness to make up their minds. The personality profile that is second in proportion among women (ESFJ) shows similar traits but in an up-front way, with extroversion. Remember, however, the influence of the last line (**J** or **P**) and how that interacts with the first line (**E** or **I**), and so be mindful that the ESFJ gal will go straight to the data – to the "facts" – and start rehearsing these loudly; while the ISFJ gal will more quietly go to how what's being spoken about will affect the people she sees as involved.

How are diferences by sex in personality patterns observed in behaviour? So what's the most obvious significance of this? It is this: for the two most common personality profiles among guys you are going to get sensory data that is treated in a rather cognitive manner. I have not said treated *well*; people can prefer a thought-through manner in a cognitive sense, but that does tell you whether they think well or think poorly, only that they prefer a thinking manner. Just recall how much half-baked and cock-eyed thinking you've heard in settings such as a hotel bar! To repeat, the most representative preference among guys is a *thinking* one. By comparison, the most representative preference among gals is a *feeling* one. This might be, "How this affects the family"; "How this affects the children" or it may be "How this keeps harmony in the workplace", whereas this will hold less sway with the guys.

One corollary of this is that often enough we will need the input of guys *and* of gals. Sometimes decisons are of a technical kind where it's usually men who've got the technical data and the technical concepts, and to include women might be "tokenism". But so often decisions are inter-personal in their ramifications, and so often women are more atune to the social aspects of what is being considered. In brief, often it's better to have guys *and* gals involved in the decision process. And often it's important for the gals to listen carefully to what the guys are saying, and for the guys to listen carefully to what the gals are saying. This is a simple application of respect for sexual differentiation (and for gender differentiation also, although I've not yet spoken much about this). This puts a rein on "put down" of the gals. But it also says to the guys, respect your guy ways, and make the best of them. But put them in context. There's a bigger picture: the world is not just populated by guys!

Some aspects of the "bigger picture". I can't go on too much on what's really a large issue. I've just focused somewhat on the differences in personality profiles by sex. But I need to reinforce that the 16 personality profile matrices that occur in the approach here presented are present for each sex. So, for example, the profile most common among adult males, ISTJ, at 16% is less common among adult females. But still about 7% of women also score ISTJ. Likewise, the profile most common among adult females, ISFJ, at 19% is less common among men, but still about 7% of men also score ISTJ. If you draw a circle and write in it GUYS, and then draw a circle and write in it GALS, then these circles are going to overlap when it comes to personality profiles. For some profiles the overlap will be more than for others, but there's overlap for all personality profile configurations. That is, variation in personality profile occurs across both guys and gals. When it comes to personality profiles, we're different by sex, but not completely different.

This kind of personality matrix overlay by sex is not necessarily a matter of confusion. You'll all recall situations such as a gal in overalls with a butch haircut and stubby fingers, and pausing for a moment to work out whether this is a gal or a guy. And, likewise, you'll all recall situations such as a guy with floppy hair and a narrow face and a rather dainty walk, and pausing for a moment to work out whether this is a guy or a gal. We can even run across kinky situations where there is real sexual confusion on the part of such a person. But mostly we fairly quickly work out whether it's a male or a female. And most of the time we need to do this sorting fairly quickly because the way we act out our personalities depends on the way sex enters the encounter. I don't give a crushing handshake to a gal, and usually wouldn't with informality call her "mate" or call a guy "dear". Our own sexual identification is hugely important for the way that we compose our personalities, and hugely important for the way we relate with the personalities of others.

But when I say "hugely important for the way that we compose our personalities", this implies that personalities are not simply "given", and that there is some development of personalities. It's to this topic that we turn in the next chapter under the title of Personality Development.

2

Personality Development

Introduction

When we speak of "development", we do not simply mean "growth". "Development" implies changes in the configuration of the personality while yet the person remains "the same person" – and in some respects "the same personality". A baby is not the same as a boy, and a boy is not the same as a man. The changes involve "growth". But, more importantly, they involve "development", while the developing person remains "the same person".

Different developmental issues are raised where psychology addresses – for example – the shifts involved from infancy to childhood, and from childhood to emerging adult, and from emerging adult to adult. In the last section of the chapter above, I shifted briefly to the language of "adult males" and "adult females" (rather than "boys and men" or "girls and women", or guys and gals). I did this because the data that I used was drawn from adult samples, and also because this profiling of personality is more applicable where personality identity is more established. That is, it is more applicable across the range of late teenagers, emerging adults, and adults (which still covers "boys and men" and "girls and women"). Further, a book like this is unlikely to be read by or to be accessible to children and early teenagers!

The point of these remarks is that "growth" such as involved in moving from "child" to "adult" is not being treated; nor is "development" being treated in the extent of "child" to "adult". "Development" as here treated covers a wide lifespan. This span can range across late teenager to emerging adult, and from emerging adult to young adult, and from young adult to mature adult, and from mature adult to middle-aged and to advanced-age adult. The point is that although the personality takes a certain profile, it yet may not be "constant", and "personality development" may occur.

The use of the permissive *may* is pointed. Some people do not develop in their personalities, and some people even regress in their personalities (and I am not speaking about the effects of senility). "Personality development" is to some extent *chosen*, and also to some extent influenced by the human environment. Readers of a book titled, *Manly Maturity*, are likely to be looking for pointers that enhance their choices in "personality development". But in order to move forward, these few points on the difference between "growth" and "development" need underscoring; the focus is on personalities that already have some stability, and the focus is on personal choice in "personality development". We can now begin to unpackage some understandings of "personality development".

What is "personality development"

A baby does not grow strong without adequate nourishment; a boy does not grow strong without adequate nourishment; and a young man does not grow strong without adequate nourishment. And, more importantly to the present argument, a baby does not develop without adequate nurture; nor a boy develop without adequate nurture; nor a young man develop to maturity without adequate nurture. These observations touch upon issues of "nature" or "nurture" for psychological development. But the point of these examples here is to draw on the sense of "strong" or "strength".

Each of us has both strong aspects in our psychological make-up and not-so-strong aspects in our psychological make-up. The way that our psychological natures get balanced-up – or do not get balanced-up – often depends upon human circumstances of nurture. I say "often", because we occasionally come across people whose well-rounded psychological make-up does not seem to be explicable in terms of their human backgrounds – people who in the face of unpropitious human circumstances develop with well-rounded, mature personalities. The importance of nurturing circumstances in personality development, or lack of nurturing circumstances and weak personality development will later be explored. And also the surprises in personality development will later be explored. But at this point I want to focus on "strength" and "strong" in the dynamics of personality development.

Strength and strong in personality development

Take the example of an adolescent boy who shows personality traits of the ESTJ kind – that is, extrovert, sensing, thinking, judging type. Such a boy will tend to be outgoing in nature; to pay attention to data of a sensory kind; tend to prefer to sort in a cognitive manner the data he takes; and tend to make up his mind fairly decisively on the things he encounters. All or any of these psychological preferences may be quite marked or may be somewhat moderate. So, for example, he may be very extrovert or mildly extrovert; very sensory in his data preference or only mildly so; very strong in preference for cognitive processing or mildly so; very decisive in his judgements or mildly so. In any event, such a young guy is going to have certain personality *strengths*. He is likely strongly to put himself somewhat up-front in social settings; likely to be able to give a strong account of data, whether it be sports scores or weather patterns; likely to show a strong preference for sorting his data by cognitive reasoning; and likely to be strong in his judgements about what needs to be done in whatever situation.

Such a configuration of personality traits is likely to put such a guy (or such a gal) in a position of leadership. If he's "too extrovert" it may put-off people, and he may be frustrated. If his judgements are too hasty, he may not take in sufficient data, and so make premature judgements. If he lacks cognitive "fire power" his cognitive processes may be defective, and others may rebutt his reasoning. That is, "strengths" can also become weaknesses unless they are tempered.

But let's for the moment proceed in terms of "strengths", and acknowledge that a guy (or a gal) of such a personality type may really gain strength in his personality identity along ESTJ lines. In short, he may become *strong*. And people may reinforce his identity strength and his performance strength, so that he both projects himself and achieves in areas that draw on these strengths. This could easily shift to a "grow" metaphor, rather than a "development" metaphor. And that's the point. "Development" involves not just "more of", but "different" in ways that involve change and complexity. Not "complex" in the sense of "I can't get a grip on this", but "complex" in the sense that it is not simply simple, but involves some subtlety, and involves movement or dynamism. But the very movement and dynamism involves growth (or better, involves development) in personality areas that are *not strong*. This is one way of looking at the dynamics of personality development.

Dynamics of personality development

People who are very extrovert are generally not very good at listening, and tend to prefer to "hold the floor". It's not helpful to tell such people to be what they are not, and to try to put them down. But for personality development it is necessary to cultivate the more extrovert person to temper his up-front-ness, and for the person himself to learn to give more space to others so that others may come forward or be drawn forward in ways that are better for them and better for the group. Sometimes this "strengthening up" of the holding-back practice can come from "hard lessons", where the over-doing it in a strongly extrovert manner has led to public disaster. But at this point, I want to emphasise a personality's *choosing*.

Choice in personality development

Generally, we can better make choices when we are strong. The extrovert who knows his strength is better positioned to strengthen his not-so-strong aspect of personality: that of being too up-front and of not reserving sufficient quiet to be more personally effective and to develop his personality in a rounding-out sense.

The same goes for "sensing". A guy may strongly like to deal with sensory data, but simply overlook or not see what is not so amenable to straightforward data gathering and processing. The man who invented the steam engine observed the lid of the kettle boiling on the stove. But his invention was not simply a matter of observation – he had an astonishing intuition. There are lots of things that are grasped by intuition, and where the psychological operation is more "intuitive" than "sensory" – although usually both are operative in differing degrees.

The intuitions usually involve dealing with *concepts*. Because concepts are abstract, dealing well with concepts requires different intelligence than dealing with what is more sensory in gathering and in processing. A higher-level mathematician will have difficulty in explaining his thoughts to someone whose mental preferences are for things that are concrete rather than abstract. Sometimes, people whose mental preferences are highly concrete are intolerant toward those whose mental preferences are abstract. For them, it can be like classical music that simply does not make sernse because it does not follow a recognisable patterning. It's in this sense that a strong "sensor" is not-so-strong.

Conversely, the person whose preferences are for intuition that deals with concepts has to learn to attend to applications and to the data gathering and processing involved in effective applications. And the guy with a strong sensory bent has to learn that he's going to need other guys (or guys and gals) who bring conceptual strengths that sharpen the gathering of data, that strengthen considerations that are not so sensory, and that sharpen the processing of data in ways that are not so readily accessed where sensory preferences prevail.

Not everyone is going to become good at this "intuitive" side of things, but building a recognition of this aspect of human psychology rounds-out the strongly sensory personality, so personality differences become better appreciated; "personality development" better proceeds; and the complementarities of personality differences are appreciated and utilised.

The same also goes with the "thinking". A guy may strongly like to "think", even while not being particularly good at it. A guy may strongly like to think in a highly deductive or logical manner. But life is not simply a set of syllogistic logic propositions. There are "reasons" that are larger than logic, as the saying, "The heart has reasons that the head knows not." This is partcularly the case in the areas of emotions and of interpersonal relations. Emotions are not simply "unreasonable", and one can deal in a reasoned way with emotions, but the manner of reasoning may be quite different from cognitive or logical reasoning. One can deal with social relations in a reasoned way, but again the reasoning may be quite different from logical cognitive reasoning. In the schema that I've used so far, this latter manner of reasoning is termed "feeling". In recent psychological literature, this is often referred to as "affect" (for example, one's feelings of affection evoke "affect", as do one's feelings of anger or of sadness). These understandings will be fleshed out in a more encompassing way in Chapter 6. But for the present, one can think of "feeling" in inter-relational terms.

Social personality development in guys

Guys tend not to be the ones who are most active in building social relations, and their social relations tend more toward "getting things done". Social dynamics often draw more upon women than upon men, and the social dynamics of women are different from men. When women come into workplaces they tend to pay attention to social dynamics to which men had not so much attended, and the workplace social patternings undergo change. Men tend to prefer to organise social patterning in terms of identified products (such as, "We're doing this; we're making this"), while women tend to prefer to organise social patterning for its own sake (such as, "It's great that our doing this brings us together in this way, and we're looking for these human outcomes in this activity").

A guy who has a strong psychological preference for "thinking" may not be very attune to what goes with those who have a strong "feeling" psychological preference. Again, the learning may be the result of collision! (even a "battle of the sexes" kind of collision!). But it may also arise from recognising that strengths also imply not-so-strong aspects of personality, and a greater readiness to accommodate those who tend differently to deal with issues, and an engaging with strengthing-up an area that is not-so-strong. This, again, involves "personality development", and usually of a "social" kind.

Guys and personality development in the judging area

The last dimension in this example dealing with an ESTJ guy is the "judging" preference. Some people seem to be like airline pilots who never land, and who seem to circle the airport, leaving others to wonder when they are going to run out of fuel! Others (and guys are more represented in this personality trait) seem in this metaphor to be in a hurry to land, and at times to make crash landings that upset themselves and others. Such crashes may be learning exercises, especially when the relevant group punishes the one who so crashes! But the learning can be self-driven and over time lead to some restraint in the disposition for closure, so that more evidence is taken and the evidence is processed more calmly and more balanced outcomes advanced. This, yet again, instances "personality development", in the sense of advancing closure or of restraining closure in appropriate ways.

From strength to weakness to strengthening

This above discussion now allows a reinforcing of approach to personality development. It is an approach that builds upon the "strengths" of the personality, and from a position of strength to attend to those traits that are not-so-strong (that comparatively are "weak"). But it involves the positioning of personality strength to deal with what is not-so-strong in order to round-out or balance-up the personality.

Another terminology for the "strong" / "weak" dichotomy is "superior" / "inferior". For each of us, some personality traits are "superior", and some are "inferior". In order to avoid put-down language, I have tended to say not-so-strong, rather than to say "weak" or "inferior". The guy who says, "I'm not very good at such-and-such, but I've learned a few tricks over the years and I'm having a go at it" is a guy whose personality is not static, but is dynamic. He's a guy who's enaged in "personality development".

The progress of this personality development starts from a certrain personality mastery that is based on a guy's strengths. That is, as I see it, personality development best proceeds from psychological strength that gives *mastery*. But this psychological mastery has a certain profile that needs to be rounded-out. The process of rounding-out or building-up involves personality development, and this leads to *progression*.

The "strength" / "mastery" / "progression" sequence is not necessarily linear and step-by-step. It can be complex. And it's not just going to be "within the person" (or "intra-psychic"). It's going to be engaged in social settings (and thus it's going to be understood in "social psychological" terms, or "inter-psychic" terms). Social settings may inhibit or advance personality development. But as I see it, the real "driver" is going to be the person and his (her) *choices*.

Before amplifying this "choice" aspect, I should reinforce that this does not involve "changing" the personality (and becoming "a different person"). It, rather, involves marshalling one's personality strengths to address the not-so-strong aspects of one's personality. This enables the person to temper the exercise of trait preferences in ways that are more helpful to themselves and to others.

A personal example may help. Some years back as Head of School I was having a difficult time with some staff members, and I remarked to my Secretary, "You know that I'm a patient man." Without missing a beat, she retorted, "You're not a patient man; you just exercise patience." I thought it prudent to make a quick retreat into my office, but I did not get the door closed before she added, "And it costs you!" She was a great Secretary, but also a great intuitive psychologist, and she taught me a lot about myself. I'd convinced myself that I was patient when really I was but exercising restraint on my drive for closure. That restraint cost me, but it also enhanced the implementation of my motive for change management in the School. Yet my personality did not change; only the way that I exercised it changed. This experience and others reinforced my appreciation that it is not so much the "personality" that changes, as modification in the ways that the "personality" is exercised. In effect, the person who undergoes "personality development" gains a more flexible mastery of his personality that gives him more *manly maturity*.

Choosing personality development

The chief actor in personality development is oneself! The person who does not want to mature will not mature. And the person who is not willing to invest in the maturation process will not mature. Whether helped or hindered, we yet substantially remain masters of ourselves. *Manly maturity* is a choice that one can make for oneself or not make for oneself. And it's not a once-up choice. In *every* era of a guy's life, new challenges and opportunities (and new hindrances) to personal development will be present. And "the present" has to be grasped in order to move to "the future", a future of *manly maturity*.

On seeking human fulfilment

Before closing this first-up approach to psychological development in its personality aspects, I should point out that while I have placed a lot of emphasis on personal choice, I also understand that personal choice in a context of grace. "Grace" is something that is unmerited. I'm a "self-made man" and most mature men are "self-made men". But if that is the sum of it, one will soon uncover arrogance. Our giftedness and our strengths, along with our limitedness and our weaknesses, are not simply "of ourselves", as our achievements are not simply "of ourselves" or of the helps or hindrances of other people. God gives grace to those who seek it. And seeking human fulfilment is a seeking for grace.

This seeking infuses life and infuses the personality in ways that merely psychogical understandings or psychological approaches do not. These remarks are to some extent a "looking ahead", because my purpose for most of this book is to portray "psychological approaches to personal maturation". But I need to alert my reader to my conviction that – for all its usefulness – "psychological approaches" are not "the whole story" in the drama of "personal maturation".

Personality Development and Developmental Psychology

The terms "personality development" and "developmental psychology" have a similar ring, but they are not the same. One can teach arithmetic to a child of normal intelligence. But one needs to wait before proceeding to algebra, and to wait further to teach calculus. Achieving this progression requires certain mathematic aptitudes or "intelligence". But quite apart from the underlying aptitudes or intelligence, there has to be a certain psychological readiness.

This readiness can be thought of in terms of stages of psychological development such as from infant to boy, from boy to emerging adult, from emerging adult to man, and even into advanced years. It is in this sense that the term "developmental psychology" is mainly used. This does not necesarily invoke development in the distinctive traits of the personality. As just briefly considered, it is where personality traits get amplified and modified around their basic configuration that we deal with "personality development". But it's well briefly in the next chapters to look at "developmental psychology" and then to look at "psychological intelligence" before moving to consider "social psychology" aspects of human development as manifesting *manly maturity*.

3

Developmental Psychology

Introduction

The human psyche is complex in both the "hard to understand" sense, and in the sense of subtle or "not simply simple". This gives rise to different psychologies that give different approaches to understanding the human psyche. The variety of approaches have a long history. Most ancient epic stories are in important respects psychological narratives. Psychology in the modern sense operates differently from earlier narrative forms and from earlier philosophical forms, and explores more empirical forms. What is presented in this chapter is highly selective from the wide array of different schools of psychology, and is directed by the need to build some foundations that are used in subsequent chapters for developing psychological approaches to personal maturation for guys – for *manly maturity*.

Developmental psychology in Freudian psycho-sexual terms

The most known name in the emergence of modern psychology, Sigmund Freud, was a medical man whose practice focused on neurotic patients, and whose psychology arose from his clinical experience and practice, which he termed "psycho-analysis". Like most early modern psychologists, this involved psychological understanding of mental disorders – and, to an extent, was "abnormal" psychology, rather than the psychology of "normal" people.

Freud's clinical experience and practice led him to explore the early lives of his patients – early lives that usually had passed from conscious awareness. And this exploration focused on their early *sexual* lives, and was in a sense "sexual psychology", and the sexual psychology of disturbed people. This psycho-analysis was an early example of "developmental psychology" in that he posited psycho-sexual developmental stages. These stages were marked by the first experience of breast-feeding through to weaning (the "oral" stage); the experience from weaning to successful toilet training (the "anal" stage); the experience from toilet training to early school years (the "penile" stage); followed by a stage of reduced sensual or sexual focus during the period of early school years through to the beginning of adolescence (the "latency" stage, or more precisely *"relatively* latent stage"); and from adolescence onward the emergence again of a "penile" stage that now was directed toward sexual relations.

Freud's psychology of neurotics – at times a psychology of abnormality or psychosis – gave an understanding of mental disorder that was grounded upon analysis of trauma or failure to resolve transitions in early developmental stages. These stages were both physiological and psychological – physiological in that they dealt with the body and growth and development of the human body (as occurs with a rush during adolescence) *and* psychological in that they dealt with psychic development in human person, particularly sexual psychology. This psycho-sexual developmental approach to human psychology will be further explored later in this book. But "developmental psychology" in the sense briefly considered in this chapter focuses not on disturbances in psychological development, nor restrictively on psycho-sexual development, but on overall and normal psychological development in a cognitive sense – the kind of psychology that informs educational practice and the normal cognitive development of the human mind.

Developmental psychology in Piagetian cognitive stages terms

Most readers will be able to recall instances of seeing children with not-comprehending, confused looks when attempting to deal with things outside their range of experience or outside their present mental development. Many readers will also be able to recall instances of persons at the other end of the lifespan where aged persons show confused, non-comprehending looks when they are unable to deal with something due to a present state of regression in mental capacity. These examples evoke appreciation of *stages* of mental development and also stages of mental deterioration. The early pathbreaker in appreciation of stages in child mental development was a biologist, Jean Piaget, whose research with children led him to posit four developmental stages.

These stages range across groupings named, "sensory-motor"; "pre-operational"; "concrete-operational"; and "formal-operational". The *sensory-motor* stage up to about 2 years of age has mental processing restricted to sensory experience such as seeing and hearing. The *pre-operational* stage spans the years of about 2 to 7, and is sparse in logic, with inadequate mental operations being confined to verbal and pictorial realms. Reasoning during this stage is primitive and is intuitive rather than logical. Thinking is egocentric, and lacks objectivity. The third stage termed *concrete-operational* stage spans about 7 to 11 years, and deals with mental operations that are concrete rather than conceptual. Examples are: "seriation" involving the sorting of objects by qualities such as size or shape; "transitivity" involving recognitions such as if object A is taller than object B and object B is taller than object C, then object A is taller than object C; "classification" as involving the ability to identify objects by defined characteristics. The concrete-operations stage also sees the beginnings of reduced egocentricism, and early growth in the ability to consider things from the perspectives of other persons.

The fourth and final Piagetian stage of *formal-operations* begins at about age 11 and continues into adulthood. This stage sees the emergence of capacity for abstract reaoning; for reasoning logically and drawing conclusions from the information available; the ability to deal with hypothetical situations; the ability to comprehend probability; and beginning to think systemically using hypothesis and deduction. In short, the entry into adolescence opens the stage of formal mental operations that continue into maturity. It also marks the entry into the fuller capacity to consider things from perspectives other than one's own – that is, the reduction in mental egotism.

The significance of this *stages perspective* of mental development is firstly in approaches to child education and child nurture. For the present purposes of considering the course of personal development from late teenage years through to mature years, the crucial point is that *before* the young person enters these maturation eras, the basic mental capacities have already undergone formation.

The foundational work of Piaget was undertaken before the advent of modern computing, but in our era we can well use a computing analogy to appreciate something that is crucial in understanding psychological development. Even without understanding computers and their operation, those who use computers appreciate the distinction between "hardware" and "software". Where one is attempting computational operations that overstrain the hardware capacities of a computer, one encounters processor slow-down in operations or operational failure. In brief, one finds a need for "hardware upgrade".

The stages of psychological development as outlined are like stage-steps in computer upgrade so that a computational system is able to move from processing simply sensory operations; to limited processing of words and images that are tied to physical objects; to more advanced processsses that yet are tied to concrete rather than abstract objects; and finally to processes that deal with objects whether contcrete or abstact in systemic and logical ways.

This analogy is stretched somewhat, because this example does not refer only to "computational hardware". The way that data are sorted systemically and logically draws upon "computational software" – that is, on "programming". If a child experiences little socialisation that nurtures consideration of the viewpoints of others, then, regardless of "hardware" development, there is not likely to be a movement away from psychological egotism. If a child experiences little socialisation that reinforces logical coherence in thinking, then mental illogicality will prevail regardless of "hardware" development. Stage progression presumes socialisation and education.

Mental "hardware" and psychological "software" metaphors

The point drawn from the foundational work of Piaget is that for the life eras considered in this book, the mental "hardware" is already in place, but the mental "software" may not be in place. One may encounter persons whose mentalities are not yet supplied with the "software programming" for effective psychologically mature operations. This does not imply that one can "buy off the shelf" a new "software package", because in this analogy the "software packaging" itself occurs by complex psychological processes that are best understood using the metaphor of building "structures" – not in the sense of mental development of a "building the brain" kind, but of psychological development in the sense of building "psychological structures" necessary for implementing mental capacity.

The psychic life of a person involves building structures that are "internal to the hardware" and that operationalise certain psychological processes. To re-state in more abstract language, the innate "capacity to learn" is in place, but we still have to learn "ways of learning": we have to "learn how to learn" and we have to learn "how to operationalise our learning". The focus then becomes not an altering of our innate capacity, but a learning how to *use* our innate capacity, and a learning how to make this learning operational in living.

Later in this book, more emphasis will be placed on

the *social* aspects of this learning and making learning operational. That is, we should not think of these processes as simply within the person (intra-psychic), but also as being inter-personal and social (inter-psychic). Nevertheless, we need to appropriate the instra-psychic aspect of our learning if we are to reinforce that personal development involves *choice*. A guy's entry to manly maturity is going firstly to revolve on *his* sustained choices for *manly maturity*.

Psychological development when basic mental structure is already in place

Eighty years after Piaget's original work, his insights still have currency. They provided a foundational grounding for experimental approaches to cognitive developmental psychology, and for the emergence of psychology based upon observational experience termed "behavioural psychology". Yet these approaches to developmental psychology, while informing the approach here adopted, are also not the primary focus for our present considerations. This is so because the present interest is in maturation across eras ranging from late adolescence to mature but not yet declining adulthood. That is, the present interest is in "developmental psychology" when from a Piagetian understanding the basic structure of mental development is already in place.

Further, a Piagetian approach proceeds in sequential stage terms, and the developmental understanding here unfolding will follow in terms of "levels", where one may encounter mobility in psychological development that at times breaks stage sequencing patterns and where in different contexts there is mobility in developmental level – a kind of practical flux or sliding up and sliding down in psychological development. Examples are where one encounters young men who have experienced schooling that has not been "boy friendly", and who when exposed to educational opportunities more suited to their psychologies seem to "jump ahead" and to make up lost ground with astonishing speed. Another example is where one encounters guys who have highly developed cognitive capabilities and skills but whose social skills seem retarded, and who have so to speak to "back track" in order properly to mobilise socially their cognitive capabilities and skills.

Intellectual psychology and social psychology in personal development

These considerations indicate that in examining processes leading to *manly maturity*, recourse is not mainly to "developmental psychology" in the sense of early stages of cognitive development; nor in the sense of marked stages in psychological development; nor in the sense simply of cognitive development; nor in the sense of behavioural psychology as learned from simulated laboratory observation. Rather, the interest is in the development of psychological capabilities and skills in the maturing human person across a wide range embracing areas that may be labelled "cognitive", "affective", "social" and "moral" – and looking across this range of labels with a sense of their interactive natures, their mobility, and their amenability to personal and social motivation in developmental outcomes.

This manner of examination positions us to move to

social psychology. But there is an aspect of the structure of mental development that still needs examining, yet to do so would overload the present chapter. This is the issue of "psychological intelligence". For the age groups addressed in this book, and accepting that the basic mental structure is already in place, we nevertheless next need to examine the issue of *intelligence*. This will be approached in a way that includes social psychological approaches to understanding intelligence. And, thus, the next chapter should again position us then to move to social psychological approaches to personal development for guys seeking *manly maturity*.

4

Psychological Intelligence

Understanding intelligence

"Firepower" is as term I like to use when speaking of "intelligence". The image is of a cannon that is going to fire misiles a certain distance according to its "firepower" – provided the gunpowder is of a given quality, is dry, the weather conditions are "normal", and the gunner knows what he's doing! These "provisos" are a bit like the "software" of the example in the previous chapter; or else like an "all other things being equal", *ceteris paribus*, proviso. The metaphor implies that there is a given technology for cannons, and thus it is cannon size that determines "firepower".

This is what it is like with scores that measure the "Intelligence Quotient", popularly termed IQ. Where the relevant "provided that" conditions obtain, the IQ scores of people can inform us of their relative psychological "firepower" – of how far in a psychological metaphor they can fire missiles. I've said "in a psychological metaphor", because I'm not speaking of the kind of response that we see when we touch a snail, and it pulls its body into its shell; nor even the activity of a bird in building a nest for its young. Such actions are not "psychological" in so far as they proceed from instinct and not from psychic learning or psychic processes. But simply voicing the "provided that" conditions brings to recognition that other considerations need to be brought to bear, whether we speak in a loose metaphor of "firepower" or are using psychometric results, IQ statistics.

What does the IQ test measure?

The first consideration is to ask, *What does the IQ score measure?* Scores for IQ tests are reported with 100 as the norm. The term "quotient" means the result given by dividng one number by another. In this case, the base numeral is an average intelligence score for a certain population cohort – say, leaving-age schoolchildren. Where the sample population is suffcently large, the sample frequency distribution of scores displays the usual "bell shaped curve" with the arithmetic mean occuring at the curve peak. Where an indiviual's score is the same as the sample mean, the resulting quotient is unity (that is, 1), and is multiplied by 100 in typical IQ reporting. Where a standard deviation is 12, then about 60% of the population falls within the conventional "normal" range of 90-109, with 20% of the population scoring below 90, and 20% of the population scoring 110 or above. Typically, a score of 70 or less indicates significant mental retardation, and a score of 130 or above indicates markedly gifted cognitive ability (that is, the top 5% of the cohort population).

Further, the standard IQ instrument generates a measure of aptitude across a cluster of mental operations typical to scholastic performance – such as mathematics, language skills, logic, spatial comparisons. Standard IQ testing taken as a whole is *not* formed to measure specific competences – such as specified competencies as used in trades such as plumbing or carpentry, or in mathematics, or in creative writing. IQ testing is intended as a score of general intellectual capability. The fact is, however, that intellectual capabilities vary. One person may have high intellectual capabilities in mathematics, another person high intellectual capabilties in language, and yet another person only average capabilities in both mathematics and in languages. Yet on a composite IQ testing, all three could have similar IQ scores. IQ testing thus scores for general cognitive abilities across the fields covered in typical scholastic curricula, and not for different competencies included in typical scholastic curricula.

From the perspective presented in the early chapters of this book, different personalities will tend to have different configurations of aptitude performance. For example, quite apart from a measure of intelligence, a "sensor" may be expected to be more attentive to observable data. In a different example, and again quite apart from a measure of intelligence, a "feeler" may be expected to be more attentive to "affect" than to sensory data. The second example has given rise in recent years to the use of the term "emotional intelligence" to convey a sense that some persons may have intelligence that is not well measured by cognitive scores. The chapter on the Psychology of Emotional Maturity explores issues raised in the second example. But we need from a different perspective to consider the limitations of IQ scores.

Some limitations of IQ scores

The recognition has already been made that IQ scores test typical scholastic abilities. People may, indeed, have high intelligence, but not in the area of scholastic abilities. Someone may become a great citizen, a great mum or dad, a great sports performer, for example, but not rank high in IQ scoring. But that's already been alluded to in what has been said above, and I amplify with some different considerations.

Variations in educational and cultural backgrounds. I remember during the first time I did an IQ test (a lifetime ago!) hestitating in the mathematics section. I'd had a poor mathematics schooling. It was not just that I am not-so-strong in mathematical aptitudes. My schooling did not well equip me to see such things as a series of squared numerals or a series of numerals increasing exponentially, and, thus, made it hard for me to make numerical recognitions. Also, the longer that I took to make these recognitions, the fewer responses I completed in the test, and the lower the overall test score. It is relevant to include the "test time", because the more intelligent a person, the quicker is response. When you've got to tell a person *twice* something that is not complex, it's a good indicator that the hearer is not quick, and cognitive quickness strongly relates to intelligence.

But what we are dealing with nevertheless remains a hard call. As a young man, I was handicapped in mathematics not so much by cognitive limitations, but by poor schooling. Those who come from home backgrounds where there is little reading and limited vocabulary may present similar limitations in word comprehension and word association. That is, even allowing for sophistication in design of the testing instrument, not everyone comes to testing with the same educational and cultural backgrounds. It is well to be mindful of the stories we occasionally hear of people who have been graded "not bright" in early years, and who later have bounced forward.

Variations in motivation. I said, later "bounced forward". More often it's a story of later "climbed forward". This touches upon *motivation*. Different personalities have differing motivations for achievement, and different persons have different experiences of encouragement or discouragement to achievement. And different personalities have differing dispositions to perseverance. These differences in experience and in disposition are likely to contribute to differing performances during the administration of test instruments. But, more to the point, they are likely to give rise to differing post-test performance. Anyone who has taught (and I have taught over many years) knows that the brightest student in the class does not necessarily top the class. Intelligence matters to achievement, but so also does *motivation*. Generally, students are not handed-back their IQ results. But anyone dealing with personal development needs to be attune to the crucial fact that innate aptitudes are *only a part* of moving forward and of motivation for improvement.

Quite ordinary people can do quite un-ordinary things when they are motivated. And quite ordinary people who are persistent also can achieve quite un-ordinary things by their *persistence*. I had a great graduate Statistics teacher, and so in a measure overcame my mathematical backwardness. Not everyone has had a great teacher or a great mentor for their area learning deficiency. I used not to have a good ear for music pitch, but I now have a very exact ear for music pitch, but I stuck at ear training over many years, simply because of my love for music.

It's really important to see aptitudes as "not fixed". There is always room for development of skills, even if it's not dramatic and even if it takes time. The message is: be patient, be persistent, but yet also be realistic.

Variations in cultural support for cognitive development. I am also convinced that a creative cultural exposure is crucial. Just tune into general conversation, whether it be on a bus, in a pub, in the school ground, or in the workplace or wherever – and it will be quite evident that unsystemic thinking is pervasive. An IQ instrument tests for cognitive cogency. Many grow up in social environments where they have limited exposure to *strategic thinking*, and experience a haphazard human world. If one has a handful of darts and a scoreboard, one acts strategically to get the maximum score. But the enculturation for many is like throwing darts blindfolded. Further, the enculturation for many does not cultivate *focus* – the simple acts of paying attention and of sustaining attention. Often it's not so much a case of "dumbness" as of lack of attention, and lack of sustaining attention. As a teacher, I used simply to stop mid-sentence when I could see that the class had lost focus. Now when I see someone is not attending to the conversation, I may just allow it to fizzle, and "move on".

Viewing intelligence in dynamic terms

What I here highlight is not just differences in aptitude, in personality, or in motivation, but also differences in cultural conditions that support processes for cognitive development as captured in an IQ assessment. In respect of ourselves, and in engagement with others, we need sharply to recognise where we need pro-actively to build the conditions for ourselves or for others to be able to enhance our intelligences.

Not all examples will be dramatic. But I experienced a dramatic example that really reinforced for me this viewpoint. I was dealing with a young man who was signalling "I want to go somewhere" but who presented a poor scholastic record. I noticed, however, that he listened attentively and with comprehension when I explained things, and concluded that he had high comprehension skills in listening. I started telling him, "You seem bright", and started tutoring him in scholastic skills. Although he had about a decade of learning to catch-up in these areas, he grew at first steadily and then at an astonishing pace – and became a high performer at university and a leader among his peers. My point is that we should look at "intelligence" in *dynamic terms*, and not simply in static terms.

An IQ score is static. It presents useful information, but it does not present determinative information. We are not necessarily going to be able markedly to increase our "firepower". But we may be able to update the technology of our particular "cannon" so that its mental capabilities are enhanced. And we may able to update the fueling of our particular "cannon" to reduce "fuel contamination" and enhance the operational efficiency of our "cannon". IQ is not fixed, and is amenable to modification by environmental interventions.

This book proceeds with this kind of perspective. "There's always room for improvement" is what you'd expect to hear from an INTJ (an introvert, intuitive, thinking, judging personality, as I am), but it's an attitude that I have also found confirmed in a lifetime of experience. We need to be realistic and only "do what we can do". But moving toward a dynamic appreciation of "what we can do" depends upon on our recognising and enacting a dynamic and forward-looking perspective.

We all face our limitations, and moving forward needs to be realistic. But it also needs to be hopeful, and dynamic. Accepting a world like a static IQ score, and seeing ourselves like a static IQ score is not "the way to go". In important respects, our psychological intelligence is dynamic.

The appeal to maturation as in the lead title of this book also applies to intelligence. We can mature in our intelligence. This may involve first reinforcing our domain-specific intelligences as a springboard for developing wider intelligences. This may involve first reinforcing our practical intelligences as a springboard for enhancing cognitive intelligence. And such an approach may involve reinforcing the masculinity of our mentality as a springboard for mental adventurousness, creativity and boldness that manifest *manly maturity*.

Intelligence is not simply "given". We are not likely radically to change our endowment. But we are able to modify and to augment its technology and its applications. We can be creative. In a sense, we can *choose* our intelligences.

We now to turn in the next chapter to the social psychology aspects of the dynamics of enhancing personal development – for us guys, enhancing *manly maturity*.

5
Social Psychology and Maturity

Introduction

Psychology as a discipline first developed with attention to the psychology of the person in an intra-psychic sense of the person. Humans are however social creatures, and so an adequate human psychology also needs an inter-psychic focus, a social psychology focus. This chapter develops one approach to social psychology and draws upon the notion of "social representation" as developed in the 1970s by Serge Moscovici, and applies this to the theme of personal maturation, to *manly maturity*.

Social Representations

This book is not substantially biographical, but it does make appeal to common-sense psychology, and one's common-sense psychology usually organises selective everyday experiences. As a means of introducing social representations, I shall relate two of these that came to my mind when I was thinking about writing this chapter. The first involved a conversation with an older woman where I was trying to convey a sense of "types" and of typology. I quickly drew the signs that now commonly appear on male and female toilets across the world. These are in outline stick-like figures with the male one drawn in "trousers" form and the female one drawn in "dress" form. This might have been quite confusing in a Victorian era when it was not uncommon for men to wear "frock coats" (and thus have a "dress-like" outline). But the il-

lustration did not "work" with this older woman. Part of
the difficulty was that "typology" is conceptual, and she
did not have a conceptual mind. But as it turns out she
had not seen or not noticed this kind of signage, such as
occurs in airports across the world. She moreover had not
thought of "types" – "men" and "women" were particular
categories to her mind, rather than "types" that might be
represented pictorially. She could little "read" the pictorial signage, and certainly could not more widely interpret
the signage in its "social representation" significance (that
is, could not "read" in the interpretative or make-sense-
of-it sense of "reading"). In brief, in social psychological
terms, she could not read the social representation that
was "outside her era and culture" and thus one that for her
did not communicate.

The second example was with a young Australian guy
with whom I happened to be walking in a city in India. He
declared, "I'm busting for a leak! I gotta find a toilet!" I
said, "Well you just walked past one!", and he looked at
me strangely as I pointed out the **WC** sign. As a child in
Australia, all train toilets were marked **WC**, and I probably recognised it was a hang-over from the Victorian co-
lonial era, and knew that it meant "Water Closet". India
sometimes retains more relics of "the Raj" than Australia,
and this young guy had never encountered **WC**, and did
not know that it was a place where you could "drop water"; that is, could urinate. He certainly could read the signage in the sense of read the letters. But he could not read
the sign in the interpretative or make-sense-of-it sense of
"reading". In brief, in social psychological terms, he could
not read the social representation that was "outside his era
and culture" and one that for him did not communicate.

These examples both well illustrate how something as simple as "This is where you can piss" involves social representation. In Victorian society, it was basically only men who could piss in public places, and one can still find in Melbourne streets some relics of the elaborate cast iron urinals for men. But in trains, "toilets" were one-person-entry only, and so one did not need any adaptation of Victorian signage for them to be used by males or females (to be "uni-sex" in a modern term). And in India, women still generally do not urinate in public places, and so **WC** often means "Water Closet" for males.

The point is that there is a culture even in something so universal and simple as urinating. And that culture is communicated by "representations" that are not mainly constructed in an intra-psychic sense but are constructed in an inter-psychic sense – in a social psychological sense. Further, this cultural construction often is sexually and/or gender differentiated. And that not simply in the sense that men usually "drop water" from a standing position while women usually "drop water" from a sitting position. In some cultures, female urination has to be less public than male urination. In some cultures, men can urinate quite publicly, whereas in contemporary Australia it requires a little discreetness – like moving to a position a bit removed from traffic and where only one's back is viewed. Most cultures however extend more liberty to men in urination than to women. But most keep urination sex-segregated – thus the now virtual universality of the "male" and "female" stick figures outside toilets.

To reinforce again the central point: a practice as universal and as simple as "dropping water" is organised culturally, and "reading" this cultural construction involves reading the "social representations" governing in this instance the act of urination.

Social representations as multi-faceted

These social representations may be in the nature of language (for example, "toilet"); in the language of picture (for example, front zips on men's clothing or signage stick-like-outline pictorial representations of a male figure); or just what one "knows" (it's okay to piss here; it's *not* okay to piss here). Further, the social representations in many things will be "gendered" (will be viewed as "masculine" or as "feminine"). One may not in cognitive terms have given much thought to such issues. But without conversance with the relevant social representations and the capacity interpretatively to read them and appropriately to respond, one would soon be in difficulty. In a metaphor, one could soon be "Busting for a leak!"

This metaphor allows mention of another aspect of social representations that is more developed in the next chapter. The language of "leak" for urination is a colloquialism that might not be "read" outside Australia, and in Australia it would not usually be used in female company. That is, there are mannerist sensibilities to be "read" in social representations, including in language usage.

In another example, I was once discussing with a visiting Religious Sister from India about the difficulties that arise there from the word "No" not being used in a negative sense. She gave me an example of where she had recently visited the dentist with another Sister who was not an Indian. The dentist had asked whether the fan was bothering her, and she replied, "No; it's okay." Whereupon the dentist turned off the fan. Later her Sister companion asked her why he'd done this when her reply was "It's okay", and she replied, "It would have been impolite to say, 'Yes', but my voice tonality indicated that I wanted the fan off."

Interestingly, "It's okay" said with a certain voice tonality now may mean among young Australians, "I'd rather not." The point is that social representations are multi-faceted, and can require complex social experience to interpret. This complex social experience involves the multi-faceted nature of the construction of social representations that should be understood inter-psychically, rather than simply intra-psychically. That is, both the construction and the use of social representations is social, and the psychology is social. The emotional (or "affect") aspects of this are more explored in the next chapter. But these remarks early reinforce that the psychology of social representations is not simply a cognitive psychology, but also an affective psychology.

Social representations as communication

From what has been said, it is evident that social representations operate intra-psychically. But it is also evident that they chiefly operate inter-psychically. Chiefly, social representations are means of *communication*. That communication may be with words (such as an affirmative *Yes* or a negative *No*); or operate by voice tonality (such as *It's okay* said in unenthusiastic tones); or operate pictorially (as in the example pictorial toilet signs); or, indeed, operate across a wide spectrum of social representation "media".

Complexity and mobility of social representations. The point is that social representations are often *complex*. And this complexity is mobile: what is fitting in one circumstance is not fitting in another; what communicates in one era does not communicate in another era. Social representations are notable for their plasticity and flux. When I answer the phone and hear, "Is that Paul?", I usually answer icily, "To whom am I speaking?" The point is that in the culture of my era only family and friends and one's "equals" may use one's familiar Christian name. But in contemporary youth culture and media culture, there is little protocol of access, and everyone is on "first name" terms, and those who do not appreciate the subtleties of this social communication intend familiarity but achieve distance. Different groups, different settings, different cultures, different eras operate with differing social representations. Communication requires an adeptess in this mobility and subtlety, and this adeptness is a cultural and inter-psychic artefact.

Personality and social representations. The sophistication of these artefacts may reflect intelligence as well as socialisation. People who are not very bright are unlikely to listen to classical music. It is too abstract and too complex for them to appreciate. I remember being shocked one time when an academic colleague said of his daughter's performances as a flautist in a Youth Symphony Orchestra, "Meaningless sound!" His remark shows that "intelligence" is not unitary, and different people have different intelligences, and he had no intelligence for music. The sophistication of artefacts also may reflect personality. Someone who is extrovert rather than introvert is unlikely to be drawn to psychology as a profession, since its practice requires a self-reflectiveness and a self-detachment in order to reflect upon the psychology of others. One thus notices a congruence between the kinds of sophistication in social representations and differences in personality. A social worker is likely to have a "feeling" personality that is congruent with building social representations of empathy with others. If pursing psychology, a sensor personality with adequate cognitive aptitudes is likely to develop social representations suited to laboratory environments and to practice a "behaviouralist" style of psychology of an academic kind. These examples are of higher-level cultural sub-sets. But social representations in general chiefly operate in "common place" circumstances.

Social representations as "common place"

Social representations mainly deal with the *familiar*. They operate to make familiar the unfamiliar. If I say of someone, "He's a good guy" this establishes a certain perspective and understanding that will influence the approach to and communication with an unknown "good guy". If I say, "He's a difficult person", this establishes a certain suspicion and cautiousness in approaching and communication with such a person. But for the social representations "good guy" and "difficult person" to operate effectively (that is, to communicate), their emergence, understanding, and use needs to be consensual. They are not the communication of an intra-psychic perception, but the communication of shared norms. Among certain higher-level sub-cultures they may be cognitive abstractions, but in general usage they are *concrete* and *commonplace*.

When an unsophisticated group of manual workers is confronted with someone who seems different and sophisticated, one of them may well say something such as "He's a bloody poofter!" This does not imply response to evidence of homosexual inclination or homosexual practice, but more simply, "This bloke is not a *good guy*. We don't think he's *one of us*." In different circumstances that may nevertheless involve ostensibly more sophisticated persons (such as a group of clergy), one might instead hear something like, "He's a *difficult person*." This does not imply response to evidence of erratic or unreasonable behaviour, but more likely that the guy concerned displays an independence of mind and a capacity for reasoning that discomforts the compromises of the clergy reference group. In brief, the exampled social representations are not mainly cognitive in nature, and they are consensual in their operation. They anchor the familiar and un-anchor the unfamiliar, and thus reinforce the *social consensus*.

Conservatism of social representations. Although social representations shift in the manners described, they nevertheless tend to conservativism, tend to assigning the preferred category, and tend to position communication in the *familiar*. In this, they tend to confirm current and common hypotheses, and tend to operate to reinforce preferred social categories. This social mentality is the obverse of the scientific mentality (whether of the physical or of the social sciences) where the method is directed to *dis*proving the hypothesis (the "null hypothesis" of statistical hypothesis testing).

Social representations as psychologically unreflective. Social representations do not cultivate neutrality. Rather, they cultivate the shared perceptions and shared and generally non-cognitive thinking. Social representations thus operate in popular culture – but also in more sophisticated culture – to give shape to and to reinforce a shared mentality. They thus give shape to and reinforce social groupings at micro-societal levels, and give shape to and reinforce social structures at macro-societal levels. As such, social representations are sociological phenomena as well as psychological phenomena. Since social representations capture and convey shared norms it is rare for them to be used reflectively. Bringing reflection to the formation and the use of social representations involves social psychic self-disclosure, and the examination at sub-strata level of the social representation or systems of social representations.

Looking at the complicity in social representations

Back in the 18th century, Adam Smith in his book *The Wealth of Nations* made the political economy observation, "Where two or three merchants are gathered together, their purpose is the restriction of trade." There of course are many varieties of "implicit hypotheses" in the many varieties of social representations, and an article on "Common-sense Psychology" found in the end-of-the-book chapter notes selectively treats that topic.

I quote Smith's general economic observation as a lead to a general psychological observation – namely, the tendency of persons and groups of persons to clothe their purposes in accepted and "respectable" terms, and the complicit self-serving nature of the implicit hypotheses to remain implicit and unexamined.

To take in turn the two examples instanced above, a group of manual workers will not usually be men of high aspiration nor men much inclined to introspection, and their work tends to physical demands and to boring repetition. Unless they are paid "piece rates", rather than weekly wages, they will tend just to do "what they need to do", and not much more. Their relevant "implicit hypothesis" is likely to be of the kind, "If the new chum disturbs our complicit work practices, it will cost us", and it is this that provokes their ostracisation.

Taking the second example, a group of clergy are likely to be men who vocalise elevated purpose but who have grown discouraged and weary as they find that anything other than "keeping the [religious] show going" brings stricture rather than rewards, and that such advancement as is possible depends upon retaining the approbation of the relevant reference group. Their relevant "implicit hypothesis" is likely to be of the kind, "Delivering according to conviction about what people *need*, rather than what they *want*, does not 'work', and disturbing our compromises ('rocking the boat') will risk our comfortable accommodations."

"Respectiability" in social representations. These instances give but psychological "spins" on the Smithian observation of the early era of the emergence of modern "social sciences". They illustrate in personal and in social terms the complicit nature of typical social representations in typical personal and group motivation and coherence. And they illustrate that it is not just "unreflectiveness" and "shared values" that tend to reinforce hypotheses being "implicit hypotheses". They illustrate the instinct for public presentation to be "respectable" and "deserving of approbation", and for the frequent disguised disjunction between the "espoused values" and the "enacted values".

Psychology of deceit in many social representations. A brief moral term for the disjunction between espoused and practised values is "hypocrisy". And on my observation, and in differing degrees, hypocrisy is endemic. But also on my observation, people and groups of people who enact hypocrisy are not very conscious that it is so. The hypocrite tends not to name himself "hypocrite", because if he did so he would feed a motivation for change, and change that could well be costly to himself and to his reference group. There is a psychology in deceit, including self-deceit, and social representations will often serve to reinforce deception and to clothe it with "good order", even with "uprightness".

Contestability in the production and reproduction of social representations. The methodology of the social sciences operates to make explicit the hypothesis and tests the hypothesis – indeed, tests to *disprove* the hypothesis (that being what the "null hypothesis" is about). This is not common-place mentality, but *contra* common-place mentality. But psychology – or at least the kind of psychology to which I tend – operates more descriptively and inductively. Psychology in the first instance treats typical psychic processes (at least for the psychology of the typical or "normal" person, rather than for the psychology of the a-typical or "abnormal" person).

Yet this "typification" is not the "whole story", since "the world" is a contestable place, and different persons or different groups of persons will offer different world-views and begin to enact different world-views. Such persons complicate the common-place psychology and disconcert the "common man" ("common man" as in the sense found in the Robert Bolt drama, *A Man For All Seasons*). The disconcerting aspects of such cultural and psychological shifts calls for refinement of social representations as these so far have been described. One such refinement is treated in the next section.

Tendency to the simplistic in social representations

Psychology as a discipline itself illustrates that "the world is a contestable place", for it is not a unitary discipline, and differing psychologies reflect differing world-views, or at least focus on different aspects of a world-view. It is useful to note this, while not here pursing the observation. My departure point is instead to notice that some people subvert stable social orders and stable social representations. Some people more readily "read" concealed complicities, and find these unacceptable or uncongenial to their own motivating psychologies. I could supply another economic example, drawing on instances such as where entrepreneurs create a new product and/or create a new market and/or reconfigure an existing product identification or product market. Or I could provide a religious example, where a religious reformer re-shapes the idealism of a religious movement, whether in terms of a "return to sources" or in terms of a "new way forward".

Such men (or such women) stand out from the crowd. Sometimes they respond to empathetic recognitions (an example from the 19th century is St Don Bosco who founded an order for the education of poor boys); sometimes they respond more to "saving one's own soul" (an example from the 3rd century is St Anthony of Egypt); and sometimes in answer to the proclamation of their salvation convictions (an example from the 12th century is St Dominic). In an unreligious age, an ostensibly "secular ideology" may be pursued. A common contemporary example is the "Green activist" whose fervent advocacy seems to substitute an ideological religious fervour, "*Save the planet!*", and whose implicit hypotheses may be as unexamined as any "Bible bashing" evangelist. The example that I shall somewhat amplify is a political one.

Broadly speaking, politics divides on a "Left" / "Right" typological scale, with modern electorates of upper and/or ascendant classes tending to the political "Right" and modern electorates of lower and/or descending classes tending to the political "Left". At its extreme, the "Left" is predicated on a distributionist (or redistributionist) conception of "the economic problem". The defects of these hypotheses have been demonstrated many times – from the de-stocking and hunger in Russia following the Bolshevik Revolution, where peasants preferred to eat their livestock than to have them collectivised, through to contemporary failures of the redistributionist Welfare States and the social distruptions caused by those who have been born into exclusion from production systems.

At its extreme, the political "Right" is predicated on a productionist understanding of "the economic problem", and the emerging new classes of the political "Right" such as seen in contemporary Eastern Europe and in China and Vietnam are dominated by entrepreneurs who generate and direct new production systems. And the political fragility of these systems is seen in the emergence of new versions of economic and political disenfranchisement and in the potentiality for flip-flop in political ideology and alignment between "Left" and "Right" and attendant political and economic instability.

Social representations and the "a-typical man"

In each case, the above broad generalisations point to simplistic hypotheses of "the economic problem" (and "the political problem"), because more complex, systemic and dynamic hypotheses are required. But in the exampled cases, the dynamic of political change (whether political revolution of the Left or of the Right) is the "a-typical man" (or "a-typical woman") who draws upon a different hypothesis from that of the earlier order and *status quo* and who articulates a "new" ideology and provides leadership for an emerging political grouping that displaces the *status quo*.

This displacement may be incremental, such as presently seems to be the case in China and Vietnam, or in discrete, such as was seen in the "fall" (or "destruction") of the Berlin Wall. The important point that I make is that such systemic reconstructions draw on a dynamic of an "a-typical man" (or "a-typical woman") and on "new" groupings for whom they and their associates act as catalysts. This is so whether in the religious sphere such as instanced by the likes of St Francis Loyola and St Francis Xavier in the 17th century, or in the political sphere such as instanced by Michel Gorbachov in the 20th century.

A crucial difficulty in respect of viability of systemic change is the requirement for complex, systemic and dynamic hypotheses to give viability to new systems. While this observation is true, it deflects from the present discussion, and the observation that system change depends upon the catalyst of the *"a-typical" person* – and depends upon the psychology of the a-typical person and the group for whom such a person is catalyst.

A-typical persons and the process of change in social representations. The general point is that the processes of change in social representations involves a contesting of dominant social representations. This challenging arises from differences in motivation and differences of worldviews and of morality. Motivation from the political Left tends arise from social empathy that focuses on the plight of the poor, and proposes the redistribution of resources from "those who have" to "those who have not". Motivation from the political Right tends to arise from the desire to create opportunity and to benefit from the fruits of opportunity by enhancing resource production and enjoying the resultant products.

Understanding contesting social representations psychologically. From a psychological perspective, these motivations differ, the social representations differ, and the moralities differ (for example, what is "just" differs between a Leftist and a Rightist perspective). But – whether from the Left or from the Right – the motivations differ from those of the earlier and *status quo* paradigms; that is, differ from the earlier social representations. It follows that the contest may be understood psychologically – in terms of differing personalities, differing psychological motivations, differing moral psychologies, and attendant differing worldviews.

Ideology in the processes of change in social representations. In the dynamics of this change, the motivating understandings necessarily take reduced-form articulation – they take *ideological* articulation. This is so because for a social representation to gain ascendency it has to gather wider support, the support of the "common man" (or "common woman" or "common person"). It has to shed sophistication, and become readily communicable. While the rhetoric of idealism may be sustained, it also has to appeal to "common interest", and usually to "common" *self*-interest. In the process, the ascendant social representation takes on the form and the dynamic of the "common place" so that it becomes "generally accepted", even "respectable". In brief, the processes portrayed in first outlining social representations find reinforcement – and there are perhaps again generated the conditions for fresh contest and displacement in social representations.

Social representations and new communications

Before moving to further exposition, there is a need to make recognition that technological changes of the present era open up new configurations of communication, and thus new processes in the emergence of social representations. I particularly refer to what is being termed as the "social media" – that is, communications that are web-based as in "Facebook" and/or cell-phone-based as in "message texting".

The application of electronic technology changes to communications technology and communications practices has profoundly altered the politics of group formation and of political activation. But it has also profoundly altered the inter-psychic processes and profoundly changed the nature of social communications.

At least in terms of catalyst-role and in terms of organiser-role, these communications changes may have diminished the role of the a-typical person in the dynamics of social change. It is probably truer to say that social media changes have diminished the role of the a-typical person in the *initial* dynamics of social change – for it is far from clear that "Facebook" and "texting" can provide the basis for sustainable and complex system change. Indeed, the very nature of modern communications – television news grab-shots, Facebook, or texting – themselves bias the social representations processes more strongly in the direction of one-line simplifications that distort rather than illuminate, and that reinforce social representations that are over-simplified – as was argued in the earlier section on the tendency for social representations to be simplistic.

Amplifying the group nature of social representations and the attendant objectification of processes

"Naming" in social representations. Social representations operate for the communication of group norms and tend to reinforce group consensuses. They operate with complicity and do not appeal to the examination of their implicit hypotheses and the presuppositions that are operative in their use. The categorisations to which they give form tend to means of social control – tend to the "naming", not least to naming the "normal" and the "deviant". The "naming" words so generated tend to objectify the "thing" named. "*That* table" or "*That* dog" does not require "objectifying", at least on a certain epistemological understanding. But "My *rights*", "His *neuroticism*", "That *immorality*" and so forth, involve an "objectification".

Social representation and the psychological identification of "things" (reification). The "naming" use of words in social representations turn the word into a "thing" – it achieves a reification. This makes a named "phenomena" such as *justice* and *injustice*, or *morality* and *immorality*, or *sanity* and *insanity* into "things". As already argued, social representations saturate the unfamiliar with familiarity, and allow the familiar to act as building blocks for a composite reality – such as the *Australian personality* or *Aboriginal culture*.

Social representations may act to conceal an arbitrariness as they endow new "existences" that are "named", and that by this naming acquire the authority of natural facts. The social representation becomes the thing represented. By a process of reification, words become what they signify. In this process, the social representations create stability and predictability and reinforce the social consensus.

This process averts reflection, averts examination of implied hypotheses, conceals complicity, conceals compromise, makes "objective" what is "subjective". As earlier argued, social representations tend to the simplistic and to the objectification of the "thing" represented.

Having traversed these observations, we may now turn to some exploration of social psychology and social representations and *manly maturity*.

Social representations and manly maturity. In this chapter I have so far said little about social representations among *guys*. That's because the very notions examined are somewhat complex, and briefly somewhat leaving aside sex and gender issues has perhaps eased the "keeping it simple" (or at least easing the complexity). But also, one should remain mindful that social representations are produced and reproduced in human societies and are both masculine *and* feminine social constructions. Nevertheless, in keeping with the theme of this book, I shall try in these last sections to give more "guy" exemplification and in its social psychology aspect more to address *manly maturity*.

Social psychology and maturity

Leadership certainly is not simply a male prerogative, but certainly *leadership* often manifests manliness. This is true in respect of manly influence in the moderation, adaptation, renewal and revision of social representations.

We have briefly seen how social representations tend to objectify the subjective, operate to support social and psychological control, and to conceal presuppositions and complicities.

The social and psychological reinforcements that thereby are operative reinforce simplistic world-views, and are easily employed to support premature judgements and early closure – in brief, to make "comfortable" psychologically and socially those whose implicit consensuses build and support the social representations.

Observations such as these may be more transparent with children than with adults. Children can be more daring and more exploratory than adults. But socially their conservatism is more evident. They prefer their established social environments, are quick to be intolerant of what they perceive as deviant, and often ready to be cruel in their exclusions of those who challenge their shared social and psychological worlds. This cruelty and exclusion can be more marked with girls than with boys. Boys are more likely to have a punch-up and soon to make-up. Girls are more likely to be spiteful and to sustain the exclusion and the deprecation, especially towards other girls.

Social representations and bolstering the psychological *status quo*. With adults, it is men who are more likely to be strongly "J" (disposed to closure and to judgement) and more strongly "S" (disposed to deal with a hands-on and sensory world, rather than an "internal" world). This is not true of all guys, but such characteristics tend to greater prevalence among guys. Taking-up the applications of these two personality traits in relation to the formation and the maintenance of social representations provides pointers toward the ways one may notice immaturity among guys in their social representations. Male social representations may in their simplisticness turn to support coarseness psychologically and socially among guys, and may support a prejudice against introspection and reflectiveness, and support crude and premature judgements of the *That's all bullshit!* kind. There are occasions for "calling a spade a spade", for "cutting the crap" and simply saying *Bullshit!* But a pattern of such behaviours is indicative of immaturity among guys.

"Working class" and "business class" instances of bolstering the *status quo*. The psychology and the behaviour just outlined might in Australian terms be called "blokesy". It may well be more noticed at the lower-end of societal structure, and partly because of the greater tendency to conservatism among "lower classes" (for example, "lower class" electorates are usually "safe" Left-leaning seats, and "swinging voters" are not much represented in such electorates). But this "may well be more noticed" may more arise from crudity of social expression. A group of men like-attired in business suits may well as much manifest unintrospective closure and premature judgement, and simply be more covert or more refined in their communication and more deferential psychologically and socially to the "boss". The *We do not see it that way*, meaning "That's not the way the 'boss' sees it"; or "That's not the way our organisation sees it" are more covert and more refined examples of *Pull your bloody head in!*

Manly leadership in dealing with unhelpful social representations. In terms of the examples given earlier in this chapter, a more mature member of a group of manual workers (a more *manly guy*) may well counter *He's a bloody poofter!* with, "Give the guy a break! He's not out to fuck you! Just give him a bit of space and let him settle-in; he's a good worker and he's not trying to push you around, just back-off a bit!"

In terms of the second example, a more mature member of a clergy group (a more *manly guy*) may well counter with, "I don't see that he's a danger to anyone; he's perhaps a bit idealistic and maybe a bit imprudent; but he's not putting us at risk; we, surely, can be 'big enough' to accommodate this guy."

These are examples of "moderation" or "accommodation" and of "tolerance", rather than distinctly of "leadership". But they are examples that cultivate a different group psychology, that moderate crude social representations, and, indeed, they are examples of responses that provide foundations for the emergence of leadership and for the revision and reform of social representations.

Refining perceptions of social representations and the attributions that are evoked

Where one is dealing with an "ordinary guy" whose self-composure gives a generosity of nature, or with an "intellectual guy" who more cognitively thinks-through what's going on and wants to respond with an open thoughtfulness, one is likely to encounter more acute perceptions of the prevalent social representations. Take, for example, the common judgement, *Where there's smoke, there's fire!* This common language encapsulates a disposition – a *shared* or social disposition – to make attributions, and typically *unfounded attributions*.

People often *want* to confirm their suspicions.

Attributions of bitter people: This tendency is particularly so of bitter people: they tend to attribute to others their own meanness.

Attributions of the sexually uptight: This tendency is particularly so of sexually up-tight people: they tend to project their own covert sexual fears on to others.

Attributions of the oppressed: This tendency is particularly so of oppressed people: they tend to suspect oppressing motives in others.

Attributions of autocrats: This tendency is particularly so of autocratic people: they tend to see any independence in others as challenging their position.

One can readily enough from memories "play back" the language used by the lackeys of a dictator against someone of independence of mind; "play back" the language of under-class groups in respect of someone perceived as a member of the oppressing class; "play back" the language that has currency among a group of "prudes" toward someone who shows an ease in matters sexual that offends their sensibilities (or in matters that are *not* "sexual", but that they with offence interpret "sexually"); "play back" the language of bitter people who attribute mean purpose to some neutral or even well-meaning word or action of others.

Sometimes what is named as "smoke" is often no more

than "mist", even the "mist" of the deprecators' own "farting". These deprecators often reveal more about those doing the "naming" than about the one "named".

The *Where there is smoke, there is fire!* involves attribution, and typically involves attribution where there is little inclination either intra-psychically or inter-psychically to engage evidentiary processes. To apply juridical language, the interest is in the *verdict* and not in the *trial*. The typical processes of production and reproduction of social representations are disposed to a "guilty until found innocent" (with an "innocent" finding unlikely!), rather than "innocent until found guilty".

Manliness in dealing with attributions. In such contexts, the manly quality of *temperance* becomes important. The qualities of a *mature* personality are dispositions to be temperate in one's judgements; to the exercise of due caution in judgement; and objectively to take and to consider evidence. And they are qualities that mark *manliness*. These qualities may be present in women (and, indeed, sometimes more present in women than in men), but in circumstances that are challenging and difficult, people tend more to look for "softer" qualities in women – for empathy, for "understanding" (empathetic understanding), and for comforting words, rather than for a disinterested disposition that withholds judgement, considers the evidence, and forms balanced conclusions systemically.

Manly dealing with not-so-strong aspects of masculine dispositions. Having so remarked, one should however retrieve awareness that not all evidence is "objective", and that evidence can also be "subjective", and that weighing evidence and thinking-through can often call upon introspection that may not be common in guys. In brief, may call upon mental processes that are not prevalent in guy culture and where recourse to different mentalities may subject a guy to negative implications from the perspective of the prevaling social representations.

This leads to the implication that *maturity* in guys (as, indeed, *maturity* in gals) calls for the development of psychological robustness that involves a certain psychological flexibility and independence. The qualities of psychological robustness may differ as between guys and gals (for example, a woman disposed to cognitive processing may attract unfavourable social representation from gals), but the more general claim about "robustness" stands. The mature guy is able "to stand on his own feet"; is able "to make up his own mind"; is able to "hold his own convictions", and so forth, in the face of crude recourse to the prevailing social representations.

Manly robustness and emotional maturity.
This robustness still calls upon a capacity to engage the psychology of others and of the group if the manly robustness is to be effective in moderating social representations, and if the manly robustness is to lead in the adaptation and reform of social representations. These last observations are developed in the next chapter on the psychology of emotional maturity and what in popular parlance has been termed "emotional intelligence". What further unfolds in that chapter is a broadening and versatility of psychological competences that are marks of *manly maturity*.

Before moving to the chapter on the psychology of affective maturity, some lighter words on an area that illustrates the fusion of social representations and the psychology of affect are in order. This is a partly fictional narrative on male costume as social representation.

A guy's dressing variety and mobility in social representations

Introduction: the context in which this text was generated. In this book I've occasional said, "I remember when", usually recalling some early memory that has taken sharper significance as I've been thinking-though and relating to the "psychological approaches" presented in this book. But readers would be amused to learn where two chapters of this book were written: on the covered deck area of a small cruise yacht along the Dalmatian coast of the Adriatic Sea! As I write, the guy in a deck chair in the sunned area in front of me has for the last 15 minutes been caressing his wife's feet! caressing rather small feet with manicured and lacquered toenails. Why do I relate this? – because it's a telling social representation of how women relish being pampered and how they'll spend a lot of time in detailed grooming, and like their bodies more than they like men's bodies, while men generally like women's bodies more than their own. (The guy had clean and unfussily clipped toenails on his stumpy feet that matched his utilitarian truck-like body.)

If you don't believe me on the last point, have a flick of the regular "women's magazines" rack near most supermarket check-outs, and you'll see page after page of pictorial representation of beautiful women for women to look at, with the guys serving as little more than "coat-hangers" over whom they may drape themselves decorously. And, incidentally, a near-naked woman on another nearby deck chair has spent a full 10 minutes without turning over the page looking at pictures of other women (the page had virtually no text thereon).

Since all the passengers but me are Spanish, with virtually no English, I've had an interesting time observing social representations that are only clothing (or un-clothing!), body language, and voice tonality – since I don't understand a word of Spanish except *Si!* Anyway, in the way that "social constructionists" read *"text"* – as another and briefer expression for social representations – the episodes being played out before me provided some interesting *text* "reading". Pity, most of the bodies carried too much fat to be quite "enjoyable", but nevertheless, I've had an interesting and enjoyable time – quite apart from the fantastic coastal setting, frequent swimming, and the lovely weather! And so, it's in this context that I give an extended personal example on "affective and emotional influences on episode representations". For simplicity, I leave implicit the other persons in the different social settings that are portrayed (other guys, gals, wife, kids, relatives, and so forth), and just talk about "myself" in a connected series of episodes in a single Sunday.

Social episodes and costume as social representations. I've chosen a narrative (a "story") to portray the variety of social episodes and congruent social representations as may be noticed in a guy's dressing.

Episode 1: the swim. The first episode is a morning

swim, and I'm wearing brief, body hugging bright blue swimmers with a white side-stripe (quite smashing, actually). I decided against wearing the bright red ones that I'd wear more if I had a bigger chest and were somewhat younger, but that seem too daring for a guy of my build and age. Anyway, the costume is a "feel good" one, and I enjoyed the swim.

Episode 2: the promenade. On leaving the beachfront, I pulled-on a pair of beach shorts, as I don't quite care for being taken as an "exhibitionist" as I walk along the promenade, but I enjoyed adopting a "walk tall" demeanour.

Episode 3: the shop. I pulled on a singlet of the "tank-top" variety before venturing down the street to buy a newspaper – again feeling I'd better not over-do my own "feeling good" mood with other customers.

Episode 4: visiting relatives. On the way home, I decided to call on some "rellies" (relatives), and swapped the tank-top for a t-shirt, anticipating the different age profiles and sensibilities in that household (and my wife's Mum doesn't care to see the tattoo above my left biceps muscle).

Episode 5: just a drop-in in smart casuals. I decided next to call on a mate who works at the local Sports Club to arrange a trip next week-end. The Club runs a "smart casuals" policy, and has a foyer sign "No thongs; No singlets" (gals seem to be exempted from the "smart casuals" policy!). I use the car back-seat as a bit of a "flex"-wardrobe, and so the t-shirt was swapped for a golf-shirt style casual top of lemon colour, and the feet got clad in a pair of sturdy sandals. It was now time to get home and get the family organised for church.

Episode 6: morning church. The weather being hot and sticky, I decided on "minimal", and changed to some more conservative shorts (less "leg" showing, and plain colour) and a subdued shirt, put gel in my hair, and contributed to getting others organised accordingly (bit of a scramble with the youngest daughter who reads all occasions as opportunity to show off her latest crazy outfit!).

Episode 7: back home. When we got back home, I kicked off the sandals (in some out-of-the-way place, I being a tidy guy), undid a couple more buttons on the shirt, and pulled it out loose over the shorts, and got myself the first beer of the day!

Episode 8: just a tad more formal social. Mid-afternoon, we had a sort-of-formal engagement, and I switched to light trousers ("slacks"), and tucked-in my shirt and reverted to only two-buttons-undone. It seemed to fit the occasion okay.

Episode 9: semi-formal social. We had to hurry home for an evening engagement, and I switched to shoes and socks for that, and a long-sleeve shirt, and checked that my hair gel still looked fresh. After a bit of debate with myself, I decided also to wear a tie, but not a jacket – though I ended up taking one to leave on the back seat of the car in case it turned out to be a bit different than I expected (or the air-conditioning was a bit cold). I certainly was happy that it was not a suit, white shirt and tie style of occasion, since I think they should be confined to Winter! I like to dress with an eye to the weather, and not just to the social representations of the episode!

Summing-up. Anyway, all-in-all it was a great day. I did not keep a tally of the costume changes or variations, but if I do so now the count is 9 (10 if you add my boxer-shorts night attire when I got home!). Well for a single day, 10 wardrobe variations is quite a lot, but across those 10 events or mini-events, I reckon that I rightly read them as 10 "episode representations", to use the term borrowed from Joe Forgas as given in the chapter notes at the back of the book.

Social world as a complex space. This story captures the sense that the social world is a complex place that is comprised of a great variety of episode spaces. It also conveys a sense that I mostly don't put on a "scientific hat" when making decisions about clothing my self-identity and giving social expression to my public identity. To borrow a jargon phrase, it's all rather dramaturgical, and the decisions are more affective than cognitive (although, being a thinking kind of guy, I often think through my affective decisions). In each episode I seemed to "get away with" my deportment decisions, and no one gave me a sense that I was "out of place" in these differering episode spaces. At some point, one of my boys said, "*Cool*, Dad!" and my wife cheerily said, "Come on 'gorgeous hunk', we're running late!"

We turn now in the next chapter more directly to dealing with the psychology of moods and emotions – that is, dealing with the psychology of *affect*.

6
Psychology of Emotional Maturity

Introduction: moods and emotions

Moods are under-lying and of low-intensity – such as a person whose mood is "breezy and light-hearted" while another is "serious". When we speak of "moody" we usually refer to a person who is somewhat "dark" in outlook and prone to be testy, and who does not much manage that "mood" – that is, in "mood" terms is neither "intelligent" nor "mature". Emotions are more spontaneous and of higher-intensity, like "happy", "frightened", "angry", and so forth. Often the distinction between moods and emotions is blurred. The psychological term capturing both moods and emotions is *affect*. In order to ease reading in this chapter, I shall avoid using the term "affect" in its more common participial function (such as, "Weather has an affect on one's emotions"), and avoid the verbal use of "effect" (such as in "It is easier to say that he 'implemented' the instruction, rather than he gave 'effect' to the instructions"). Both moods and emotions can be thought of as an *array* of affective or non-cognitive capabilities, competencies and skills that impinge upon one's life performances.

The full range of moods and emotions occurs across guys and gals, and so it is difficult readily to treat emotional maturity only in masculine terms as *manly affective maturity*. Some typifications as between masculine and feminine psychologies as so far been considered will be noticed later in relation to the consideration of affect. But the focus has first to be on understanding more generally the psychology of affect, before some generalisations may be drawn in respect of *manly affective maturity*.

Emotional intelligence and personality

There continues to be a debate as to whether there is such a "thing" as "emotional intelligence". The "answer" depends upon the kind of psychological perspective adopted. This book opened with the presentation of an essentially Jungian psychology of personality. In this perspective, we "arrive" with a certain personality configuration that manifests itself in certain psychological preferences of the "extrovert" / "introvert" kind, the "thinking" / "feeling" kind, and so forth. From this perspective, our psychological development first proceeds along lines congruent with our psychological preferences or strengths. It follows that different configurations of psychological competencies are observed. But, as argued in the chapter on Personality Development, our psychological strengths offer leverage for our developing the not-so-strong aspects of our psychological aptitudes.

This perspective, however, was not used to argue that all psychological aptitudes will be equalised or that we all will become equal in all psychological aptitudes. That this is not the case was argued in the chapter on the Psychology of Intelligence. We pretty much have a given intelligence endowment (what I colloquially term "firepower"), and some have more firepower than others. But, to sustain a mechanical metaphor, mechanical performance depends upon more than engine capacity – "gearing" also greatly influences performance. And so with psychological performance, a person of lesser firepower who has more "learned to think" and to think systemically can demonstrate higher intellectual performance than someone of greater firepower who has less "learned to think". And, further, someone who is motivated to "think" will think more than someone who is not so motivated to think, regardless of whether the person has more firepower or less firepower.

The Jungian psychological paradigm is not the most popular one in Psychology, at least in academic psychology, and – as I see it – the general lack of adherence to a Jungian perspective contributes to certain deficiencies of perception in a number of psychological discourses. This is so in respect of the psychology of moods and emotions (or in the jargon preferred by psychologists, the psychology of *affect*), and in discourse about "emotional intelligence".

Differing personality preferences for affect and cognition. Affect in the Jungian approach that I favour is popularised under the label of "feeling", with "feeling" being understood at least as much in inter-psychic terms as in intra-psychic terms – indeed, probably mainly in social psychological terms. This means that different people will have different preferences for *affect* ("feeling"), while others will have different preferences for *cognition* ("thinking"). But this does not mean therefore that the person who prefers cognitive thinking is weaker in affective thinking than the person who prefers affective thinking to cognitive thinking. Such a comparison depends upon *relative* intelligence – upon who has more firepower or who is "brighter" across the various psychic domains. And, yet further, this depends not simply upon "endowment" in a static sense of psychological intelligence. It depends upon psychological development – in the typology of the present discussion, upon cognitive psychological development and/or affective psychological development.

Environment and motivation in affective and cognitive development. Affective and cognitive psychological development will depend upon external circumstances such as the relevant *cultural environment* (for example, one cultivating mental logicality or one cultivating a mentality of harmonious social relations) and upon *motivation* (for example, whether one wants to develop one's "intellect" or to develop one's "affect").

Moreover, environments are not "givens" – one can modify one's environment or one can move to a different environment. And motivations are not "given" and may shifts according to opportunity, mood, or health, and so forth. All these points thus reinforce that "emotional intelligence" is not a "given". Like other psychological aptitudes, "affect" also can undergo development.

"Development" also can be regressive ("He hardened his heart") or progressive ("He has become a more feeling person"). Where affective development is viewed in positive terms, the language of "emotional maturity" or of "emotional maturation" may be used. The psychology of moods and emotions had a fillip of interest with the popularisation of the notion of Emotional Intelligence. This term has a "static" ring about it, and this chapter treats the topic in "dynamic terms", as reflected in the chapter title, the Psychology of Emotional Maturity.

Emotional Intelligence may be defined in the following terms:

> The ability to recognise emotions, to identify the meanings of emotions and their relationships to reasoning and problem-solving. This evokes the capacity to *perceive* moods and emotions; to *assimilate* moods and emotions; to *understand* moods and emotions; and to *manage* moods and emotions both within oneself and with others. Where this range of aptitudes and competencies may be scaled, tests of "emotional intelligence" may be generated. Whether formally scaled or not, it is across this range of senses that we can speak of "emotional intelligence".

Intelligence and its affective and cognitive development

From this discussion, it may be seen that I do not subscribe to the view that Emotional Intelligence is simply an aspect of Personality Psychology – although it of course is not unrelated to Personality Psychology. Thus, persons with a psychological preference for "feeling" are more likely to develop intelligence in moods and emotions, just as persons with a psychological preference for "thinking" are more likely to develop cognitive intelligence. But I return to my earlier metaphor of "firepower", and where the psychological preferences of a person are not supported by innate "firepower", the "feeling" person is likely to be more "emotional" than "emotionally intelligent". Similarly, where the psychological preferences of a person are not supported by innate "firepower", the "thinking" person is likely to manifest "crude thinking" or "confused thinking" that does not attract the label "cognitive intelligence".

Reinforcing, however, a non-static or developmental approach, social environments that manifest emotional stability are more likely to foster "emotional intelligence", in much the same way that educational environments that cultivate careful thinking are more likely to foster "cognitive intelligence". Not that "cognitive intelligence" and "emotional intelligence" should be set one against another – rather, they should be considered as components of a broad-based perspective of "intelligence".

Composite nature of affective intelligence.
One of the lines of argument in the chapter on the Psychology of Intelligence was that "intelligence" is a composite faculty and capacity. The "IQ" of "Intelligence Testing" was developed to test scholastic aptitudes that are akin to cognitive intelligence. Some people suggest that "Intelligence Testing" should be expanded to comprise a wider range of psychic aptitudes and competences.

What is probably more apt is that intelligence tests should be crafted for the purposes for which they are intended. For example, it does not follow that someone who does not score high on an IQ score should enter a Trades Course, rather than a University Studies. Trades such a carpentry and electronics typically require aptitudes such as manual dexterity and arithmetic competencies for preparing job quotations and specifying supplies requirements. They are better thought of as "different intelligences". This implies a need for wide-spectrum aptitude testing for "vocational advice" purposes (what jobs would seem to suit your aptitudes and competencies?), with wide-spectrum aptitude testing followed by targeted aptitude testing for more defined purposes.

In a restricted professional sense, "emotional intelligence" is going to be far less relevant for someone embarking on a course in Mechanical Engineering than for someone embarking on a course in Social Work. When it comes to practical applications, a Mechanical Engineer with poor "emotional intelligence" is however not likely to move into Management areas in an organisation, while a Social Worker with poor "cognitive intelligence" is not likely to deal well with the complexities of regulatory environments that nowadays are the context for higher-level social work practice. It remains the case, however, that different aptitude and competency configurations will have different congruencies with different personality types and different congruencies with different occupational categories.

Role of motivation in affective intelligence.
As with "intelligence" in the conventional "IQ" sense, so with "emotional intelligence", performance outcomes are not simply a function of inherent aptitudes, but also a function of conscious development. No matter how "bright", a mentally lazy person will manifest a mental slackness. The "brightest" are not necessarily the best performers in the class. This is also the case with affective intelligence, because its manifestation requires a conscious development that gives rise to *conscious self-regulation* in the affective area.

This conscious self-regulation spans areas such as *conscious awareness* (or "paying attention" in matters of affect); *self-reflection* (or intra-psychic considerations of affect); *self-regulation* (like "controlling one's temper" or "moderating one's crossness"); and *will* (pursuing responses that are affectively appropriate).

To further illustrate these four dimensions, one can often notice a person who simply does not care to exercise an *awareness* of others' affective responses, and so offends. One can often notice a person whose busyness is of an avoiding *self-reflection* kind, and who ends up repeating affective offence. One can often notice a person who exercises little *self-regulation* and continues not to restrain affective responses that affectively offend others. And one can often notice a person who does not seem to *will* moderation of affective responses that affectively offend others.

All these examples point to the centrality of *motivation* in the conscious self-regulation of affect. People who are not motivated to moderation of affective responses "don't care" to notice; "don't care" to examine matters of affect; "don't care" to restrain affect in themselves or in others; and "don't care" to implement in matters of affect.

Such people are "shut off", "unaware of themselves", "out of control", and "wilful" in respect of their un-moderated affective responses. Such people will be "emotionally *un*intelligent". But this is not necessarily because of deficiency in inherent aptitudes. It may be because of lack of motivation to develop affective intelligence. This conclusion is of course a value-laden one. It implies a person who is blameworthy in the area of affective behaviour, and not simply "unintelligent".

Non-dichotomisation of affective and cognitive intelligences. A sharp dichotomisation of "affective intelligence" and "cognitive intelligence" is not helpful. Affective influences on everyday thinking, judgement and behaviour occur because the way that we *feel* is inseparable from the way we *think* and process information. There is a fundamental interdependence between "feeling" and "thinking" – between affective functioning and cognitive functioning. An "intelligent person" is one who integrates psychologically both affect and cognition.

In order, however, to advance the topic of this chapter, we concentrate further on the psychology of affect, and how affect can enhance or inhibit psychic poise and performance.

Role of affect infusion in affective intelligence and cognition

In this treatment, I draw somewhat on recent work by Joe Forgas as acknowledged in the chapter notes at the end of this book. A key interest in this approach to affect is what Forgas terms "affect infusion". An example is that persons in a positive mood are more likely to access and to recall positive information and information that was first encountered and processed in a positive mental state. By contrast, persons in a negative mood are more likely to access and to recall negative information and information that was first encountered and processed in a negative mental state.

This means that affective state impinges upon or "infuses" the integrated psychic responses of affect and cognition. Becoming aware of such often subtle and unconscious psychic effects is an important part of affective or emotional intelligence. This is perhaps particularly so where the emotion is high-intensity and urges attention on the focal aspects of some situation or some issue, and gives rise to emotional *un*intelligence. Emotional intelligence constrains this kind of obsession and evokes consideration of all features of some situation or some issue, and allows the integration of affective and cognitive components in psychic response. Further examples of how affect influences the psychic responses include:

what we notice;

what we learn;

what we remember;

and the kinds of judgements and decisions that we make.

Affect infusion can make fragile the judgmental and decision processes. Awareness of affective states builds emotional intelligence and thus allows more integral judgmental and decision processes.

There are however some refinements to be considered, and in this I further draw on the arguments of Forgas and Wyland on affect infusion and social behaviour – treating both its functional and dysfunctional aspects. And in so presenting, I shall again draw on the Jungian perspective first introduced in the chapter on the Psychology of Personality.

Personality and affect infusion

We first turn to the affect infusion in its dysfunctional aspect where moods and emotions bias perceptions, decisions, and relationships. Conscious effort and awareness are required to correct dysfunctional affect infusions. The capacity to marshal this effort and to sustain awareness of affective biases are marks of "emotional intelligence".

The need to marshal the effort and to sustain awareness

of affective biases varies with the kind and context of perceptions, decisions, and social relations, but also with the speed of decision-taking. For example, most product advertising is directed to appeal to affective states and to prompt quick decision. The very quickness of decision that most advertising prompts reduces defences against affective distortions in judgements. This leads to "mis-wanting", imprudent choices, even to folly. But the relationship between speed of judgements (quick, or considered) and affective distortion in judgement is not so simple. This relationship varies as between positive affect and negative affect, and whether affect is mild ("mood") or intense ("emotion").

Mild negative affect lowers affect infusion.

Mild negative affect generally produces more careful and externally-oriented processing styles that are more attuned to the requirements of a given situation. For example, the "bright and breezy" personality who brings a positive mood to a given situation is more likely to allow positive affect to infuse situational decisions. By contrast, the "serious" personality who brings a negative mood to a given situation is more likely to be led by low-intensity negative affect to adopt a more careful and externally-oriented processing style that is more attuned to the requirements of a given situation. That is, the person who brings mild negative affect is more likely to take further evidence – including non-intra-psychic evidence – and thus more carefully to adjudge the evidence before moving to a decision and to enacting a decision. In brief, the less "sunny" personality type is more likely to manifest "emotional intelligence" and disinterested decisions.

I should remark on my use of the term "disinterested". Nowadays, even in literature where the author should know better, one notices confusion between "uninterested" and "disinterested". The person who is "uninterested" has no motivation to engage the issue, and is simply "not interested" or has low-level "interest". The person who has motivation to engage the issue but who wants to adjudge the issue responsibly is "disinterested". Such a person searches the issue, considers the variety of aspects of the issue, and forms a judgement that does not necessarily reflect the self-interest of the person, but gives a "disinterested" assessment and decision. It is like a juridical process, where impartiality is expected of the judge and where the decision does not reflect the interests of the person making the decision. In assessing examination papers, I used so to fold the front pages so that I could not see candidate names, in order to assess the papers "blind". This practice reflected a mild negative affect – that I did not quite trust my own mood in relation to individual student performance, and this gave rise to practical cautions against affective contamination of my judgements.

Strong negative affect heightens affect infusion. An obverse outcome occurs where negative affect is intense. Strong negative emotions prompt a more intra-psychic response than inter-psychic response, and the result is the heightening of projection of intra-psychic states upon the external environment. Persons with strong negative affect do not rely upon open memory-based thinking and objective data in the formation of their responses.

It is important to be able to discern the fact of psychic projection, because at times considerable subterfuge may be used in concealing this psychic projection. Take, for example, an extensive and data-laden consultancy report for government that opens with the phrase, "Climate change is the greatest threat facing mankind today, and perhaps ever." This immediately signals a lack of knowledge and/or understanding of history and an awry view of contemporary human challenges: it immediately signals a precept that is "affective", rather than "objective" – and immediately signals a disposition to manipulate data to support a prior conclusion that derives from an affective state.

Deceit in concealment of affect infusion. At times, the signaling may be less immediate, and one may need some astuteness to discern affective contamination of "research" processes and outcomes. One may need a careful eye to see how "evidence" is being manipulated to support a "conclusion", but where the "conclusion" is really the motivation for the research activity. In such cases, the research activity is simply a screen to meet social norms and/or legal requirements, but not an activity of "disinterestedness".

Personality and deceit in affect contamination. A variety of personality traits may impinge upon this kind of deceit. There may be a marked lack of introspection such as occurs with strong sensor ("S") personalities combined with strong motivation for closure as occurs with strong judging ("J") personalities. Where socially-accepted processing requirements require concealment of actual motives, then a major "research" project may be embarked upon. Often such "research" projects will display weak intuitive aptitudes and competencies, and so their speciousness will be evident to an attuned reviewer. Where the issue is more conceptual as in philosophical and/or theological issues, such "research" tends to display astonishing syllogistic tightness, along with a marked exclusion of varieties of research paradigms and approaches, especially a marked exclusion of inductive reasoning rather than deductive reasoning. Again, to an attuned reviewer the speciousness of such approaches will be evident.

Where the reviewer is read in the psychology of emotions, this speciousness may be identified in psychological terms as "affective contamination" of process and outcome. Person engaging such specious research efforts may be "intelligent" in a cognitive sense of intelligence, or they may be "unintelligent" in a cognitive sense of intelligence, and quite unaware of how transparently specious is their "research" activity. Unawareness of this kind may be reinforced by ostensibly following supposed "process rules" and by assurance that comes from "backing from the boss".

More on covert affect infusion. Such "research" activities can thus be engaged by seemingly quite different personality types. A cowardly and not very bright sycophant to "the boss" or an ascendant clique may so act. Such a person may have so little introspection as to be unaware of the measure of affective contamination and the hypocrisy involved in the specious "research". But also the "gung-ho" missionary type who is quite bright and committed to a "missionary" cause (whether secular such as "climate change" or religious such as "evangelistic") may so act. Again, a lack of introspection may leave the "missionary" quite unaware of the measure of affective contamination and the speciousness of the "research".

Where the negative affect includes deep resentment, even hatred, the motive for concealment of the true intent of the process may be increased, especially when the "I want to 'get' this person" is not socially acceptable. Where the negative affect includes vaunting pride, the motive for concealment may be increased, because simply "*I* must not be wrong!" is usually socially unacceptable. One needs to be able to "read" not only the "affective contamination", but also the style of "social representation" that is employed to *interested* purpose – *affect interest* purposes that compromise disinterestedness in psychic processes, decision, and action.

Affect and the psychology of social exclusion. The above paragraph treats more "formal" social representations. More typically, we deal with less-formal social representations. Gossip is a prime example. A person or people start "farting", and say *Smoke!* and then, "Where there's smoke there's *fire!*" This then gets followed with the gossipy building of circumstantial evidence to give credence to the "fire" behind the "smoke". Then social ostracisation comes to force and the "smoky" person gets isolated and no one (at least no one who "counts") transacts with or listens to the person who is traduced. The traduced person becomes an "outcast", and, unless that person is strong psychologically, behaviour that seems to give credence to the gossip begins to be seen, and the gossips begin to feel vindicated. Unless there is someone with affective maturity and/or institutions that uphold affective maturity, then the intense negative affect dominates. The result is contaminated individual and social decisions and actions that are harmful to all concerned.

There is another scenario that highlights the need to assess affect contamination in relation to the personality. In subjects who have a strong judgement preference ("J") and who prefer to process sensory data ("S"), strong negative affect will be directed exteriorly – that is, it will be projected upon others. Others will be blamed:

"they" will be *stupid*;

"they" will be *non-conformist*;

"they" will be *blameworthy*, and so forth;

while "me" and "us" will be praiseworthy and the negative affect and behaviour of the "S,J" will be interpreted in socially-acceptable terms (will be given a favourable "spin"), and will be acted out in position-congruent social representations (such as "What men in our position would do"). That's the scenario portrayed above. But for persons with opposite personality traits, marked negative affect is worked-out quite differently.

Another side of personality and affect contamination. In someone whose psychological preference is "intuition" rather than "sensing", strong negative affect actually inhibits accurate perceiving and processing, and may even shuts-down accurate perceiving and processing. This leads to the intra-psychic response of introversion, even extreme introversion, and closing-off of communication. The capacity accurately to assess "what's actually going on" is seriously impaired and sober estimation of the circumstances and functional responses to the circumstances are inhibited. Rather than act soberly to deal with the circumstances, the tendency is to portray catastrophe (to "catastrophise"), and the subject may "take flight" – seek "surrealistic" data or experiences that relate poorly to the current project and/ or "crisis" and opt-out of the situation, rather than face the situation.

An alternative scenario is covertly to decide to "have a breakdown" – to induce psychological collapse in the hope that someone will take pity and/or someone will come to the rescue. In such persons there may be an appearance of judging ("J") behaviour, because decisions may be made quickly. But this arises not principally from the judging trait in the usual psychological sense – for such judgements are typically self-harming and socially-damaging, and typically are not assented to by the subject after calmer reflection. What we encounter is the behaviour of an un-sturdy personality under stress. For such persons, the counsel needs to be "Decide nothing; do nothing" until this is thought through, and thought through with a calm facilitator. In psychological terms, where the intra-psychic contamination of negative affect is heightened, the subject is prone in one way or another to *self-harm*. This is the obverse of the more typical case, where marked negative affect operates in the first instance to *harm others*, rather than to harm the psychological actor.

Mild positive affect lowers affect infusion.

Looking now from the perspective of positive affect, those with mild positive affect may enhance a "bright" social outlook. But it is unlikely to be significant strategically. Such people are unlikely to be strategic leaders, because their mild disposition does not dispose them to see the "darker" side of issues, to process "darker" side considerations, and to formulate and enact in respect of "darker" issues, whether intra-psychic or inter-psychic. Such people tend not to be identified as "emotionally intelligent", and will rarely manifest personal maturity or exercise leadership. Although not particularly "useful" from social perspectives such as strategic organisational development, such people nevertheless tend to be harmless socially.

Strong positive affect heightens affect infusion. By contrast, those with strong positive affect tend to be harmful socially. This is the kind of person who also does not take evidence, but is quite dogged in not taking evidence – and so the "facts of the matter" are ignored and/or denied until it is too late to retrieve the situation. Simple examples are the mother who will not see the dysfunctional behaviour that she has induced and is supporting in her emerging-adult or adult son, or the starry-eyed young man who will not see the diminishing behaviour of the young woman with whom he is infatuated. Another example is the "happy clappy" type who just does not deal with the realities of life until collapse is upon him. Evidently, such persons lack "emotional intelligence".

Informational and processing aspects of affect

We need now to move toward some integration of the topic. The starting point in building emotional intelligence is an awareness that affect can have a powerful influence on the way that people think and act in social situations. Forgas and Wyland identify two kinds of influences, "informational" and "processing".

Informational influences occur because affect informs the content of memories, thought, judgements, and actions. *Processing* influences occur because affect also informs how people deal with social information. These affective influences on judgements and behaviours are highly content specific. Also, as argued, the dynamics of affect on judgements and behaviours are much influenced by personality as well as social context. Gaining a comprehensive appreciation of this complex of influences engages the processes involved in becoming more "emotionally intelligent".

Affect congruence and emotional maturity.
As emotional intelligence matures, the subject is more able to promote or to inhibit affect so that there is an *affect congruence* with the person or persons and with the situation. That is, an appropriate measure of "brightness" may be introduced into an unhappy situation, or more "hopeful" affective response in a seemingly hopeless situation; or, alternatively, an appropriate measure of affective "seriousness" may be introduced into an "all's well" situation, or emotional "alarm bells" sounded in a situation of potential crisis, and so forth. The perspective of the present discussion does not comprehend all aspects of affect, but it does provide occasion to observe the importance of "affect congruence" in the maturation of emotional intelligence. This may be thought of in terms of "effort" and "manner of processing".

Manner of processing affective influences.
Effort refers to the measure of investment in affective attention and processing. *Manner of processing* refers to the quality of attention and processing. The first refers to quantity, the second to quality. In respect of the quality aspect, Forgas proposes a fourfold stylisation of manners of processing affective influences:

Substantive processing involves high effort and open and constructive consideration of affect.

Motivated processing involves high effort and closed and restrictive consideration of affect.

Heuristic processing involves low effort and open and constructive consideration of affect.

Direct access processing involves low effort and closed and restrictive consideration of affect.

Direct access processing. There are many circumstances when *direct access processing* is the most appropriate course – such as where one needs to take a low-level and small-consequences decision that simply involves the retrieval of existing and already-processed information. There are many everyday decisions where people need to make quick and largely unreflected social decisions. There are some instances where accuracy indeed depends upon direct access processing: completing a Personality Questionnaire needs to be done mostly unreflectively if it is to give raw data on personality preferences. More considered responses may actually distort preference revelation and so distort the profiling of personality traits.

Motivated processing strategy. *Motivated processing strategy* is suited to some circumstances, where there is highly selective and targeted information search and information processing that is dominated by a particular motivational objective. But there are strong hazards with this manner of proceeding, and it is less likely to manifest emotional maturity. This is the kind of processing strategy that delivers "What I want" or "What the boss wants" or "What the prevailing clique wants" or such as "Conforms to the current manner of thinking and opinion". An example is how you decide to conduct yourself in a job interview.

There are hazards in adopting this model – one may find oneself in a conformist situation that is ultimately uncomfortable, even soul-destroying. This manner of processing may be heavily subject to affect infusion of the kind such as "Must please the boss; must please the teacher", "Must not 'rock the boat' and upset people" kind. One needs a keen sense of the kinds of social representations and the processes of constructing and maintaining social representations in order also to read into these the affective dynamics, and to moderate these affective dynamics in order to achieve affect congruence.

Heuristic processing strategy. *Heuristic processing strategy* is likely to occur where the task has little personal relevance and where there is no need for detailed processing. It's a kind of "How do you feel about such and such?" processing, where the matter of question is not of much significance or not of much significance to the person. This kind of processing is of course more subject to affect infusion, but this contamination of response may not matter much.

Substantive processing strategy. *Substantive processing strategy* best fits situations where people need fully and constructively to deal with social situations. This is an inherently open and constructive thinking style that most characterises our most personally relevant and important decisions. It is here that affect congruence is most important, and where affect incongruence is most dysfunctional. Effectively to implement this processing style draws upon affective maturity and characterises those with aptitudes and accomplishment in "emotional intelligence" and who integrate affective and cognitive intelligences.

Reinforcing the influence of personality on the disposition to affect contamination. We should underscore the observation that positive affect promotes a more internally-driven and top-down thinking style. The more extrovert ("E") and more judging ("J") personality is more likely unwittingly to succumb to affect contamination when engaging in unfamiliar, complex, and a-typical tasks – and thus is more likely to project his affective dispositions upon the task at hand. Conversely, the more introvert ("I") personality with a moderate judging function (mild "J") personality is more likely to tend toward negative affect and thus less likely to succumb to affect contamination when engaging unfamiliar, complex, and a-typical tasks. This is because the greater congruence toward negative affect in such personalities promotes in such circumstances a more externally-focused and bottom-up thinking that generates careful research and wider-ranging reasoning that is congruent with a mildly negative affect status.

Processing strategies in affect management. The implication of these considerations is that affect management can involve recognition by persons of the need to switch processing strategies between the different forms – so as better to calibrate their prevailing moods and/or emotions to the thinking and action tasks at hand. Thus, differing use of differing processing styles may constitute a dynamic and self-correcting means of managing mood and emotion so that affect states are more congruent with the differing situations and the challenges that are faced.

Affect in a cross-cultural perspective

Among the behavioural attributes that we expect of a "mature person" are that he is not "racist" or "sexist". This is not to say that different races do not in general have different aptitudes, nor to say that males and females do not in general have different aptitudes. It is to say that where one is dealing with a person, one should be wary about attributing to a person the aptitudes and/ or behaviour that appear to be more prevalent in one class or another (such as where "race" or "sex" present the class grouping). The same applies with "culture". While recognising this, I want to make some generalised observations on cultural differences with respect to "maturity".

"Maturity" as encultured. The observation is that "maturity" and "intelligence" in a personalised sense are really "encultured" terms that arise from a certain cultural environment where "personal identity" is more individuated. In a sense, this is not a "modern" phenomena, for in reading history we encounter persons of marked "personal identity" who were weakly conformed to prevailing cultural norms.

Although there is much "identity conformity" in modern "Western" societies, our societies nevertheless do uphold a view of "personal identity" that has a certain "modernity" and a certain increased congruity with modern Western societies. I have experienced teaching in non-Western cultures and among students from traditionalist cultural backgrounds – and it is difficult to communicate to such students that it is *critical thinking* that I want, not reproduction of "what the lecturer says". But the equivalent of "what the lecturer says" remains culturally prevalent across much of the world, especially in cultures that emphasise not "the person", but "the rank that the person holds" or "the rank into which the person was born", and so forth.

A non-teaching example of this will often be encountered by air travellers between Europe and Australia during an Asian transit stop. The present world aviation protocol is that hand luggage cannot contain liquid or gel in containers of more than 100ml. The specification is *container capacity* – rather than content – presumably because some containers are inflexible and/or not transparent (that is, one can't by feeling and/or viewing assess how the full or otherwise is the container). One can be pretty sure in Australia that where a 150ml container is obviously only half-full, it will be waived on, because in Australian culture there is a greater assumption that the "intention" should be observed, rather than the strict "letter", and an interpretative judgement is likely quickly to be made in a relaxed manner. Not so in Asian airports.

No matter how obvious it is that the container has less than 100ml of liquid or gel, it will be taken from the transit passenger, and usually done so in a supercilious and abrupt manner as a matter of "law". Any challenge about the reasonableness of such action is likely to be met with a sulky disposition reflecting that challenging is an affront to the "face status" of the policing officer. This is an example of *im*maturity in encultured norms.

Mature and immature cultures and cross-cultural comparisons. Behaviours that are unrefined in their rule-based applications and that do not admit challenge are "immature" from the value premises that are evoked in a *personal* sense of "maturity". But the point that I am making is that some *cultures* may set up as "norms" behaviours that from the normative position followed in this book would be regarded as "immature".

This presents difficulties in terms of mature approaches to "cross-cultural psychology". It would be a mistake to make the attribution that cross-cultural awareness and/or cross-cultural tolerance will resolve conflict issues of this kind. Such awareness and tolerance will not suffice, because – from "our" cultural viewpoint – certain behaviours will be anger-making, and will be dealt with openly. From "the other" cultural viewpoint, the converse behaviour will be anger-making, and may be accompanied by a refusal to deal openly with the issue.

Sometimes, the only "way out" is simply "cultural avoidance" – like, "Do not buy any duty-free item until you re-enter Australia." But if one in psychological terms has to answer, *Why?* a frank answer may be:

Because in some cultures persons less have a "personal identity" and more have a "class identity", where "class identity" and "class behaviour" tend to be inflexibly rule-based and where conflict is usually dealt with covertly and on a "class norms" basis. In psychological terms, this is not "mature", and the behavioural manifestations of this "immaturity" will be anger-making from "our" understanding of "maturity".

Such statements would doubtlessly be "politically incorrect", but from the normative position followed in this book, they accurately describe situations that can be understood from a "cross-cultural" perspective, but in person-to-person terms will generate psychological conflict and actual conflict of a kind that "psychological maturity" (on "our" part) is not necessarily going to resolve.

Psychological maturity is no "fix all". These specific examples serve to introduce a general point – namely, that "psychological maturity" is not in itself necessarily going to make life easy or calmer. When an adult behaves like a child, it will still be anger-making. When an officer acts unnecessarily officiously or defensively, it is still going to be anger-making. When someone who ought to exercise some common sense in interpreting a rule, but is unwilling and/or psychologically unable to do so, it will still be anger-making. When something needs to be dealt with openly, but is dealt with only covertly, it will still be anger-making. Simply being "mature" is not in and of itself going to make life more pleasant. One might perhaps be more dexterous in navigating difficulties of this kind. But one might not be "more dexterous", because "He's just doing his job" may be diminished as a shrugging-off of issues that need to be faced, and one may think and feel more acutely that "his job" should be done more reasonably and more intelligently and more considerately.

"Maturity" is not a "fix all" for life's difficulties that arise from different psychologies – whether these arise from influences such as cross-cultural differences, male/ female differences, or inter-generational differences.

"Maturity" can help, but it does not necessarily resolve the fact that life throws up many conflicts and these conflicts are sharper where the psychologies of the persons differ – especially where differing intra-psychic and inter-psychic structures of behaviour are incongruent.

Emotional maturity and manly maturity

This chapter is already somewhat long. Rather than further test the patience of my readers, more direct outlining of its implications for manly maturity are found in the Overview Perspectives chapter. From what has been argued in earlier chapters, it should be evident that the psychological range of normal personalities – both male and female – means that different guys will face different challenges in developing the "affect management" aptitudes needed for personal maturity.

The emphasis in this chapter on the non-dichotomous nature of affective and cognitive reasoning leads naturally to considering in the following chapter the more cognitive area of "moral psychology". There then follow chapters that trace some of the challenges that guys face choosing against *immaturity* to act with *manly maturity*.

This manner of proceeding prepares the way for the later Overview Perspectives chapter that treats the integration of cognitive and affective maturity among guys.

7

Moral Psychology and Maturity

Morals, ethics, values

Because terms such as "morals", "ethics", and "values" need to be unpackaged in order to speak about "Moral Psychology", it is necessary to spend a little time attending to some words and word meanings used to develop the ideas in this chapter. A little patience is also asked of readers before moving to Moral Psychology *and Maturity*, and beginning to develops this in terms of *manly maturity*.

My early reading in graduate Psychology was in the area of Social Psychology in organisations – usually labelled Organisational Behaviour or Organisational Psychology. It took a while before I had an *Aha!* moment. That moment was when I first recognised that the term *values* was being used differently.

I had no issue with the term "value" in the sense of "price" (that drink is priced at $5; its "value" is $5). It was the term *values* that was being used differently. In my mind the collective term, *values* meant something "objective" – like, "My values are such that I could not endorse trafficking in humans, because I don't believe that people should be bought and sold." Where I was speaking in terms that I regarded as "*not* objective", I tended to use language such as *preference* or *taste* – like, "I don't much care for smorgasboard meals, as I prefer to take one dish for my main meal", or "In considering cars, I do not look at them as just 'transport', because I have a taste for cars, and enjoy a car that I find beautiful." I thus tended to reserve the term *values* for "more serious" usage. When speaking about things where reasonable people could reasonably differ I still generally prefer to use the language of *preferences* or *tastes*.

Values. But in the Organisational Behaviour / Organisational Psychology that I was reading, the term *values* had a different sense. For example, things such as "consultative management styles", "merit-based selection", "equal opportunity", were presented as organisational *values*. I valued such things, and I guess I'd have just used a term such as "organisational policy" for such things. What I realised is that these *values* were not specified or understood in terms inherent to what was being spoken about – they were not spoken of in "objective" terms. Rather, they were spoken of in terms of what was common agreement within the organisational culture ("shared values", or "implicit values"), and different organisations could have different "organisational values". Alternatively, these policies might not be shared within the organisation (not be "shared values", or "implicit values"), but instead be specified in documents with a title such as "Staff Procedures and Protocol Manual". Organisations whose values behaviour was governed by such Manuals were termed "low culture organisations", because not governed by implicit, shared values as found in what are termed "high culture organisations". Where behaviour was consistent with such shared values or with values articulated in such managerial documents, it often attracted the labelling "ethical behaviour".

Ethics. We now often hear used without explanation

terms like "ethical behaviour" or "ethical practice" in matters as diverse as "privacy policy", "human tissue use in hospitals", and "financial disclosure". Sometimes when we are presented with outrage media coverage there is an appeal to implicit values that are also objective – such as rape crimes. Often, however, this is not the case, and in these instances we tend to hear terms like "unethical", "unethical behaviour".

I want to take up this language and apply the term *ethics* to that to which people give assent or to which those who govern give assent. In so using the term *ethics*, I do not ascribe some "inherent value". I simply make the ascription that this is:

- what is commonly upheld in a given culture (be that a modern corporate organisation or in a typical family setting) or
- what is enforced in a given culture as "appropriate" behaviour.

Such "ethical behaviour" may have an inherent "rightness" or it may not have an inherent "rightness". In the usage I am adopting, *ethics* may be viewed as "cultural practice", and I differentiate this from *morals* and *morality*.

Morals. This distinction is simply a convenient one, because the words *ethics* and *morals* have similar root meanings in their original languages — *ethics* having come into English from Greek, and *morals* having come into English from Latin. But the English terms *morals* and *morality* have somewhat gone out of fashion. They are unfashionable because "This is right" and "This is wrong" tend *not* to imply "This is my view" / "These are my values" or "These are our views" / "These are our values". That is, the language of *morals* now tends to convey a sense of *right* and of *wrong* that is not viewed as a matter of opinion, consensus or common practice, but of something that is viewed as inherently *right* or *wrong*, something that is *good* or *bad, virtuous* or *evil*.

Such a view potentially diminishes the "Me" and the "Us", because "I" and "We" are constrained by the inherent qualities of *rightness* or of *wrongness*. Compared with the use of the term *values* in the way that I first formally learned in graduate Organisational Psychology, a *morality* approach tends to collision with the values of contemporary culture. This clash arises because we live in a culture where "relativist" values prevail – where people believe that they can choose their values much as they might choose their "lifestyles".

Re-stating it more simply

All this could get far too complex for the purposes of this chapter. I raise it because my readers will bring a variety of perspectives to what is to be discussed. Some will mainly view things from the "ethical" perspective as outlined, others will mainly view things from the "moral" perspective as outlined. For myself, I think that some things are but matters of "taste" or "preference"; and some things are more serious and matters of "ethics"; and some things are yet more serious and are matters of "morals". And some things are all three things: things I "prefer" (or do *not* "prefer") *and* things that I think "ethical" (or think "*un*ethical") *and* things that I think "moral" (or think "*im*moral"). That is, we can deal with "overlapping sets", where the three categories are not quite separate.

Commonly, however, "overlapping sets" will differ in their "overlap", so that an issue may have elements that are matters of "preference", *and* elements that are matters of "ethics", *and* elements that are matters of "morals". It then becomes a question of how I *mainly* consider the issue. If I consider the issue *mainly* to be "moral", this is likely to influence the reasoning process. Sometimes "moral" issues can be straightforward, but often they are *complex*. Adequately dealing with issues that are complex calls for higher-level reasoning, and higher-level reasoning does not just "happen": it is the result of processes, *psychological processes*. These psychological processes are possible only where a *psychological structure* has been built.

The building of psychological structures typically occurs in social contexts. Sometimes people form their minds interiorly ("intra-psychically"), but mostly people form their minds in social contexts ("inter-psychically") by processes that fall under the general label of Social Psychology. I mainly view Moral Psychology from a Social Psychology viewpoint. The more robust and refined these psychological structures, the more mature is the Moral Psychology. The more masculine in character these psychological structures, the more the Moral Psychology befits a *manly maturity*. But I must ask of readers further patience in dealing with conceptual issues before being able to develop these conclusions in the two following chapters.

Moral psychology

There are two reasons why I have adopted the term Moral Psychology, rather than some term seemingly more accommodating to contemporary society. The first is that my interest in this chapter tends toward the higher-level reasoning that more readily attaches to the label *moral*. The second is that the term Moral Psychology was used by Lawrence Kohlberg in the 1970s and by William Kurtines in the 1980s in their pioneering work in this area. I now turn to outlining aspects of their approaches that are relevant to the theme of this book.

In the classical sense of the terms, *ethics* and *morality* have long histories from their Greek and Latin antecedants. Moreover, the intense philosophical debates on *morals* of recent times engage the philosophical backdrops in the development of Moral Psychology and the critques of its development as a sub-discipline of Psychology. Dealing with these philosophical backdrops would involve complexity and contention. Readers who are educated in Philosophy will identify certain philosophical perspectives in what has already been said. For the most part, I will not try systemically to treat these philosophical issues, and more address the topics in psychological terms.

Moral Psychology as developed by Kohlberg draws on a Piagetian understanding of Developmental Psychology as earlier outlined in the chapter so titled. This is captured in Kohlberg's key use of the term "stages" in his seminal book, and his presentation of the psychological stages as sequential. There are three levels in the Kohlbergian schema, each with two sub-levels, giving the six stages. He terms these levels: "pre-conventional", "conventional", and "post-conventional".

Pre-conventional "morals". The "pre-conventual" level has a sub-stage of *obedience and* *punishment orientation* ("How can I avoid punishment?"), followed by a *self-interest orientation* ("What's in it for me?"). Contrary to a Kohlbergian position, it is hard at times not to see regression from later stages to what in Piagetian terms are childlike earlier stages – because evaluations that are childlike in their psychology seem too often to operate in the behaviour of adult persons.

Conventional "morals". The "conventional" level has a sub-stage of *interpersonal accord and conformity* ("The good boy conduct" / "good girl conduct"), followed by *authority and social order orientation* ("What are the rules?"). Again, it's hard to see that there is no regression from later stages to these earlier stages, as it's not only adolescents who submit to peer pressure, and it's not only the morally naïve whose recourse is simplistically to "It's the law!". As I argued in my treatment of Developmental Psychology, a perspective of *mobile* levels rather than of sequential stages often better fits psychological behaviour.

Unlike Piaget whose focus was on earlier years, the Developmental Psychology of Kohlberg takes a more human life-span perspective, and thus more directly addresses psychological development across different life eras. From the perspective of this book, it is the third "post-conventional" level that is most relevant, with its sub-stages of *social contract orientation* ("social consensus formation") and *universal principles orientation* ("principled conscience").

Post-conventional "morals". The "post-conventional" level sub-stage of *social contract orientation* necessarily builds social psychological processes in the formation of psychological structures for moral choice – and thus necessarily encompasses Social Psychology perspectives in the formation of moral judgement. But the Kohlbergian perspective is somewhat inflenced "top-down", and so within the "post-conventional" stage, it is the second and last sub-stage of *universal principles* that most informs this Moral Psychology perspective and takes it decidedly in a Cognitive Psychology direction.

Critique of Kohlbergian "principled moral psychology"

In a sense, such a Cognitive Psychology direction is reasonable, as moral choices involve *reasoning*. However – as has earlier been alluded to with the phrase "The heart has reasons that the head knows not" and as was developed in the chapter on the Psychology of Emotional Maturity – there are styles of reasoning that are not so simply cognitive. Further, moral reasoning as developed along Kohlbergian lines gives a psychological reading of the principles of justice philosophy as developed in the 1970s by John Rawls – and is thus somewhat Rawlsian. This approach focuses in a rationalistic way on principles that are seen as *universal* and on *justice as fairness*.

It is probably true to say that *justice as fairness* has wide appeal – virtually the first moral cry that one hears in school playgrounds is, "It's not fair!" This, however, does not capture the range of considerations of justice that people deal with. Further, the individualist contractarian perspective in this "social contract" approach to justice does not capture the range of situations in which people adjudge what is just. Certainly those coming from a perspectives of "leftward learning" political philosophies will not be convinced of the universality of a Rawlsian perspective. This rationalist perspective has also been challenged as being "masculine morality" by those who see women as bringing different perspectives to moral reasoning. I expand consideration of these issues shortly after considering another shortcoming in Kohlbergian approaches to Moral Psychology.

As noted, the prevaling contemporary approach in Moral Philosophy and in Moral Psychology tends to focus on *principles* and *process*, and not on the moral decision itself. There is a lack of focus on questions of a "right" / "wrong" or "virtue" / "vice" kind, where *good* and *bad* are appraised in essentialist terms – in terms of whether in and of itself some behaviour should be adjudged *right* or *wrong*. Given the "post-modernist" and relativist leanings of Westerrn societies since World War II, it is not surprising that intellectualist Moral Philosophy and Moral Psychology should reflect such a perspective.

In dealing with the divide of (a) the "appropriate" / "inappropriate" and (b) the "right" / "wrong", many people without recourse to sophisticated reasoning support moral stances with the rhetorical question, "Am I infringing anyone's rights?" Yet, however, many people when scandalised and without much sophistication will voice, "It's just *wrong!*", and convey an essentialist sense of moral choice: that some choices are in and of themselves right, and some choices are in an of themselves wrong. From a Kohlbergian perspective, these voicings could be regarded as but "conventional" – as "social norms" from a social constructionist perspective or as "rules" from a law and order understanding of morality. How does one get around this quandary?

Further spects of "over-lapping sets". As I see it, my remarks about "overlapping sets" provide a perspective. Some choices reflect "likes" and "dislikes". Some choices reflect social norms, and are adjudged "ethical" when they do, and "unethical" when they do not, and in current usage the terms "appropriate" and "inappropriate" have a fashionable ring. Other choices engage the inherent morality of what is being adjudged. Where an inherent morality is identified, "principles" and "process" are not going to suffice. We may need recourse to principles and processes as a manner of proceeding, but they are not the final arbiter. The final arbiter becomes reasoning in the *moral* sense that I have described.

Yet, however, the issues being adjudged often will not fall into one of the three categories or another. And some people will see the issue as mainly of one kind (such as social contractual, "What is acceptable behaviour?"), while others will see the issue as mainly of another kind (such as, "This choice is immoral, and it violates what I regard as fundamental!"). In such cases, reasonable negotiation may lead to reasonable compromise. Adjudging the acceptability or otherwise of such compromises brings dilemmas that raise complex issues of moral reasoning that may or may not lead to moral assent.

Building psychological structures for moral discernment and decision

We have to recognise that moral choices are often complex and often messy, and require higher-level reasoning – and not solely cognitive reasoning – to form moral judgements. These higher-level reasonings do not just "happen". Psychological structures have to be built to sustain higher-level reasoning processes, and not least higher-level reasoning processes that involve discriminating "preferences", "ethics", and "morals". This structuring process may be viewed as Developmental Psychology under a heading of Moral Psychology.

Where these structures are poorly developed (and where, in an earlier metaphor, the "firepower" is weak), we may use the term "moral immaturity". Where these structures are complex and refined and with consonant active psychic processes, we may use the term "moral maturity" (or having maturity in Moral Psychology). Higher-level moral reasoning is not simply a matter of greater "firepower". Much depends upon *motivation* and *persistence*. Maturity in moral psychology is not the prerogative of an intellectual elite. Ordinary people can "sort" quite a lot – sometimes using formal categories, sometimes more intuitively and without formal categories. But without the effort of building psychological structures a mature moral psychology is unlikely to emerge.

The psychological make-up of men and women are not entirely distinct, but as I have earlier argued are "over-lapping sets". Within the complex of psycholgical characteristics we nevertheless encounter clusters that tend to be more present in women than in men, and other clusters that tend to be more present in men than in women. That is, from a maculine perspective we may identify development in moral psychology that is aptly named *manly maturity*. This viewpoint is perhaps contentious, and I shall begin to amplify this perspective in the section that closes this chapter and to apply it in the two subsequent chapters. To lead into this I shall draw upon a social cognitive psychology approach to moral thought and action.

Social cognitive theory and moral psychology

This section draws on the psychology developed in the 1980s by Albert Bandura on the social foundations of moral thought and action. Necessarily, the presentation is greatly abbreviated. The Social Psychology approach developed by Bandura takes up the Kohlbergian stages framework: punishment-based obedience; evolving though opportunistic self-interest; approval-seeking conformity; respect for authority; contractual legalistic observance; and culminating in principled morality that is based on standards of justice.

Role of cognitive dissonance. From this perspective, changes in stages of moral reasoning are provoked by cognitive conflict arising from exposure to higher levels of moral reasoning. Judgemental standards of lesser complexity than those already embraced are supposedly rejected, because they have already been displaced by higher standards of thinking.

Exposure to moral reasonings that is too discrepant from one's dominant stage of reasoning have little impact, because they are insufficiently understood to activate any change in reasoning processes. Alternatively, where advanced reasoning processes are too divergent from one's established reasoning processes, they may fail to activate changes in moral reasoning. Sometimes this may arise because the test of maturity in moral reasoning may more reflect one's preferences than competence in moral reasoning. For example, there may be instances where social regard and concern for others (stage 3 moral reasoning) may seem more viable than one rooted in law and order (stage 4 moral reasoning).

Moral reasoning from a Kohlbergian perspective is staged with regard to the *form* of reasoning, and not to its *content*. But the *form* of moral reasoning does not ensure the superiority of its *content* – does not ensure superiority of actual moral judgements.

Context considerations. Bandura evidences the common finding that adults comprehend different moral principles, but use them selectively or in complementary ways, depending upon the interplay of circumstances and the domain of functioning – that is, according to *context*. Moral development produces multi-form moral thinking, rather than follows a single developmental track. For example, whether people offer principled solutions for moral conflicts may reflect not the competence of their moral reasoning, but more reflect their perceptions of the gravity of the consequences that they perceive. Furthermore, the moral judgements of people typically rely on reasoning from several different moral standards, rather than being based upon only one line of moral reasoning or only one formulation of moral standards.

Sensitivity to divergent considerations. As I have written elsewhere (see chapter notes), one may have moral reasoning that is syllogistically tight, but that does not deal with varieties of evidence and varieties of contexts. This at times is the case in received Moral Theology reasoning where a certain tight logic prevails, but where there is weak traction with empirical evidence or practical concerns and practical applications. The moral reasoning – *content* – may be quite high-level, and yet weakly address divergent concerns and divergent *contexts*. That is, the cognitive level of reasoning alone does not ensure a moral robustness. Bandura sums up saying that the mature mode of thinking is characterised by sensitivity to these divergent factors that are morally relevant in any given situation. Often, choice of judgemental standards depends – partly, if not wholly – on which factors are most germane to a particular moral problem.

Social influence upon moral action. Judgemental standards often test people's moral courage. One observes how children learn to discriminate between approved and disapproved forms of conduct ("nice" and "not nice"), and regulate their behaviour on the basis of anticipated social consequences. Adults likewise often regulate their behaviour according to social expectations and the degree of social stricture, rather than according to reasoned judgements of the rightness or otherwise – *content* – of their behaviour.

Bandura speaks of the power of social modelling in influencing standards of behaviour. This occurs not just passively in terms of responding to social influences. People respond interactively to construct behavioural standards from the numerous evaluative rules that are prescribed, modelled, and taught. People often display inconsistencies between what they practice and what they espouse, and such behavioural inconsistencies – whether designedly or unintentionally – complicate the socialisation process. In brief, espoused values are not necessarily practised values.

Continuous processes in building values.

Decisions about how one responds to the disjuctions between values and practice involve higher-level discriminations. Such discriminations are only possible where the person has constructed a moral identity that is one's own. This involves the building of mental structures that allow the mental processes involved in weighing complex issues. This then allows the bringing together of complex issues enabling a prudent exercise moral courage in decision and in implementation. This involves intra-psychic processes, but also inter-psychic processes of social learning. These are continuous processes by which behavioural standards are elaborated and modified, new standards are adopted, and the effective communication of one's reasonings and actions is achieved in the relevant contexts – communication that usually will require dialogue, "dialogic processes".

Motivation in moral thought and action

Sustaining these processes necessarily engages *motivation* – motivators for cognitive development in moral principles and values, and motivators for acting morally. Standards alone do not drive actions. Indeed, if disparities between perceived events and mental structures were actually automatically motivating, everyone should be highly knowledgeable about the surrounding world and continually progressing toward ever higher levels of moral reasoning. The evidence does not seem to bear this out. For many people, cognitive dissonance often seems to have little impact upon moral reasoning. The more potent motivator for producing changes in moral reasoning seems to be the experiences of coping with social discord arising from issues of morality. From a Kohlbergian perspective, higher-level reasoning exercises more motivational appeal than lower-level forms of reasoning.

Development of moral reasoning. It is common to observe that people tend to be unaffected by mental processes that are below their dominant mode of thinking, and are more likely to adopt a decision model that is one stage above their own ("more likely" to adopt, not *will* adopt).

Some people both in terms of their personalities (intra-psychically) and their social contexts (inter-psychically) are more strongly resistant to change in mental processing. Kohlbergian researchers find evidence that the more discrepant from one's views is persuasive reasoning, the more one's attitudes change. Cognitive limitations and immaturity of course place limits at any life-era on the power of discrepant influences. Further, conflicts have to be filtered, otherwise daily lives would be overwhelmed by innumerable imperatives for cognitive change. Effective functioning requires selective deployment of attention and enquiry.

Moral judgements as application of multi-dimensional rules

In the social cognitive view, moral thinking is a process in which multi-dimensional rules are used to judge conduct. Situations with moral implications contain many decisional ingredients that not only vary in importance, but also – depending on the particular constellation of events in a given moral predicament – may be given greater or lesser weight. Among the many factors that enter into judging the reprehensibility or otherwise of conduct Bandura lists the following:

- the nature of the transgression;
- the base rate of occurrence and degree of norm variation;
- the contexts in which it is performed and the perceived situational and personal motivators for it;
- the immediate and long-range consequences of the action;
- whether it produces personal injury or property damage; whether it is directed at faceless agencies and corporations or at individuals;
- the characteristics of the wrongdoer, such as age, sex, and social status; and
- the characteristics of the victims and their perceived blameworthiness.

This is a complex list of multi-dimensional factors that could easily confuse the mental competency of many people. It is clear that experience and development in cognitive competence are required for moral judgements to change from single-dimensional to multi-dimensional rules of conduct.

The more complex rules involve configural or relativistic weighing of morally relevant information. In the cognitive processing of information regarding the morality of conduct, people will tend to be influenced in modelling the rules both in form and complexity by their reference group – with children their parents, with adolescents their peer group, with adults the dominant social reference group. Where the dominant social reference group focuses attention on informational complexity and situational variation, this tends to cultivate relativist and situational "morality" – what I earlier termed *ethics*.

The less cognitive and less essentialist, and the more *affective* and more perceptualist, are the values of the moral actors, the less one encounters strictly "moral" decision and action – and the more one encounters "ethical" decision and action. And in these situations, "scandal" is likely to be provoked by action that infringes relativist and situationalist "codes of conduct" and to be conventional – rather than essentialist – in its evaluation and response.

Such conventional responses may implcitly be used to build an affective environment of social control aimed at achieving conformity with largely unexamined and inter-psychic "values" that function to reinforce what become commonplace and group ethics – a kind of club mentality that governs conduct and assures conformity with group or social norms. Thereby, "scandal" ceases to be a moral category, and becomes instead one of social and affective sensibilities. That is not to say that there is not a place for such subjectivist social norms, and the section on "Social episodes and costume as social representations" in Chapter 5 provides an example. It is, however, to say that such considerations do not treat "morality" proper, nor do they provide the stuff of "scandal" properly understood.

In scenarios where social subjectivist norms prevail in regulating human conduct, ostracism then operates to conform behaviour for ends that have little to do with upholding personal or social *virtue* – since it is "safe" conformity, rather than integrity, that drives these inter-psychic behavioural patterns. Such behaviour fits a psychological pattern for making opaque disjunctions between implicit values ("implicit phlosophy") and espoused values ("explicit philosophy"), and for concealing the hypocrisy that this disjunction entails.

Contemporary culture tends against moral reasoning. Social psychological processes as just outlined are magnified by the very complexity and diversity of contemporary "Western" culture that tends to find against concluding outcomes that are essentialist or *moral* in reasoning. As Bandura expresses it, social consensus on morality is difficult to come by in everyday life. This creates ambiguity about the correctness of moral judements.

In the absence of consistent feedback, reliance on convenient heuristics may become routinised to the point where moral judgements are rendered without giving much thought to indivuating features of moral situations. The susceptibility of moral judgement to change depends in part on the effects of the actions it fosters. Over time, people alter what they think by experiencing the social effects of their actions. This leads us to consideration of the relationship between moral reasoning and moral conduct.

Interplay of personal and social sanctions

People may act pro-socially or transgressively out of mutual obligation, for social approval, for duty to the social order, or for reasons of principle. The level of moral development of the person may indicate the types of reasons likely to be most persuasive to the person, yet the level of moral development does not ensure any particular kind of conduct. The form of reasoning may be indicated by the stage of moral development, but not the morality of the conduct – although the higher the level of moral reasoning, the more likely is moral conduct, and the more likely is a greater consistency between moral judgements and conduct.

Affective influences in moral reasoning. Affective factors play a vital regulative role in moral conduct. Self-regulation of moral conduct involves more than moral thought. Moral judgement sets the occasion for self-reflective influence. Affective self-reactions provide the mechanisms by which standards regulate conduct. The anticipatory self-respect or self-censure for actions that correspond with, or that violate, personal standards serve as the regulatory influences. People do things that give them self-satisfaction and a sense of self-worth. Ordinarily, they refrain from behaving in ways that violate their moral standards because it will bring self-condemnation. Self-contempt often acts severely as punishment for moral failure. Anticipatory self-sanctions thus help to keep conduct in line with internal standards.

Triad of behaviour; cognition; environment: an inter-actionist perspective. The self-regulation of conduct is not entirely an intra-psychic affair as the more radical forms of cognitism might lead one to believe. Nor do people operate as autonomous agents impervious to social realities in which they are enmeshed. Following Bandura, social cognitive theory presents a causal model involving triadic reciprocal causation. The three constituent sources of influence – (1) *behaviour*; (2) *cognition and other personal factors*; and (3) *environmental influences* – all operate as interacting determinants of each other.

From this interactionist perspective, moral conduct is similarly regulated by a reciprocal influence between thought and self-sanctions, conduct, and a network of social influences. After personal and social standards of self-reactive functions are developed, behaviour usually produces two sets of consequences:
• self-evaluative reactions, and
• social effects.
These two sets of consequences may operate as complementary or opposing influences on behaviour.

Conduct is most congruent with moral standards when transgressive behaviour is not easily self-exusable and the evaluative reactions of significant others are compatible with personal standards. Under conditions of shared moral standards, socially approvable acts are a source of self-pride, while socially censured acts provoke self-censure that acts to inhibit socially transgressive behaviour.

To enhance the compatibility between personal and social influences, people generally select associates who share similar standards of conduct, and thus ensure social support for their own system of self-evaluation. Thus, the diversity of standards in a society does not necessarily create personal conflict. Selective association can forge consistency out of diversity and foster virtuous development in moral psychology or alternatively support comfortable stasis in moral psychology.

Such "comfortable stasis" in moral psychology may reinforce ethical positions that are formed by affective dispositions and/or reinforce moral positions that are formed by syllogistically tight cognitive positions that are weakly contextualised. In either case, the selection of associates who share similar standards of conduct may operate to form "comfort clubs" or "mutual admiration societies", rather than to form socialisations that foster maturity in moral psychology and probity in moral enactment.

Behaviour is especially susceptible to external influences in the absence of countervailing internal or intra-psychic standards. People who are not much committed to personal standards adopt a pragmatic orientation, tailoring their behaviour to fit whatever is called for by the situation. They become adept at reading social situations and guiding their actions by expediency. Such guys (or gals) are "followers" in matters of taste, ethics, and morality, and exercise no leadership. In moral psychology terms they remain *immature*.

Conflict between self-approval and social-approval

One type of conflict between social and self-produced consequences arises when individuals are socially punished for behaviour they highly value. Principled dissenters and non-conformists often find themselves in this predicament. Here, the relative strength of self-approval and social censure determines whether the behaviour will be restrained or expressed.

Should the threatened social consequences be severe, people hold in check self-praiseworthy acts in risky situations, but perform them readily in relatively safe settings. There are, however, individuals whose sense of self-worth is so strongly invested in certain convictions that they will submit to prolonged mistreatment, rather than accede to what they regard as unjust or immoral.

People commonly experience conflicts in which they are socially pressured to engage in behaviour that violates their moral standards. When self-devaluative consequences outweigh the benefit for socially accommodating behaviour, the social influences do not have much sway. However, the self-regulatory conduct operates through conditional application of moral standards. Self-sanctions can be weakened or nullified by exonerative moral reasoning and social circumstances. People display different levels of detrimental behaviour and offer different types of moral reasons for it, depending on whether they find themselves in social situations that are conducive to humane conduct or hurtful conduct. But almost any conduct can be morally justified, the same moral principles can support different actions, and the same actions can be championed on the basis of different moral principles.

Adherence to moral conduct cannot be simply attributed to "maturity", nor immoral conduct simply to "immaturty". Nevertheless, "immaturity" does in several respects provide a suitable banner under which to examine immoral behaviour and unmanly behaviour, and the banner of "immaturity" finds some application in the following two chapters.

Manly behaviour
and moral psychology

It is fashionable nowadays – especially in academic studies – to decry differentiating behaviour between men and women as "sexist". Where this involves applying some "stereotype" or some "average type" to particular persons, then this may well be negatively discriminating behaviour on the basis of sex, or "sexism". Women are often more emotional than men, but not all women are "emotional". Men are often less expressive in their emotions than women, but men in general are not thereby "unemotional", and not all men are emotionally restrained. The very way in which the term "manly" is used in this book alludes to a favoured set of masculine qualities – qualities of masculine maturity that are gathered-up in the later chapter devoted to Manly Maturity. Only some central generalisations from this discussion of Moral Psychology are now briefly noted before moving on to selective wide-ranging and sexual issues of immaurity among guys.

Summing-up. A key central point to reinforce is that development in Moral Psychology is not simply a "cognitive" matter. One has to be careful not to see "affective reasoning" as the domain of gals, even while recognising that gals often show more adeptness in developing and demonstrating affective reasoning. A manly Moral Psychology tends to give emphasis to a strength in cognitive structuring and cognitive processing. But such strength will be "gender stereotyped" – rather than manly – if affective reasoning is not integrated into a guy's psychological structuring and processing and behaviour. The fact, however, remains that psychological development typically proceeds from one's strengths and from using one's strengths to even-up one's not-so-strong aptitudes. Guys needs to affirm their psychological strengths in ways that over time round-out a psychological maturity, a *mascultine moral maturity*.

Content *and* context in moral enactments.

Such manly moral enactments do not occur in a vacuum, but in contexts. In the contemporary relativistic context of "postmodernity" there is a heightened danger of *context* being emphasised to the detriment of *content* in moral reasoning and behaviour. Finding the right balance involves both manliness and womanliness in psychological development and behaviour, and this balance is mainly not achieved in sexual isolation. Yet guys need to identify and to pursue psychological development in manly ways that integrate content and context in moral reasoning and in moral enactment. The desire to grow into and to enact a masculine nobility is central to the motivation of guys to engage in the psychological development necessary for thinking and acting with manly moral maturity.

Sometimes the negative ("What *not* to do") can be more telling that the positive ("What to do"), and the two following chapters include psychological approaches on "What *not* to do" to the under the banner of *Immaturity among Men*.

8
Immaturity among Men: wider-ranging issues

Introduction

Chapter headings need to be snappy, and this chapter heading does not quite capture the chapter content. "Men behaving badly" was a working heading. But the book, although encompassing behaviour, is about "psychological approaches to manly maturity". That is, the book is not simply about "behaviour", nor simply "behaviouralist" in its Psychology. Where treatment is of unfavoured attributes, a Moral Psychology approach might proceed under a "Men behaving badly" flag. Terms such as "manly" and "maturity" are normative ones in the sense of suggesting favoured attributes, and the book focuses on ways of understanding and cultivating these qualities among guys. This chapter thus highlights certain unfavoured attributes among guys and how these may be countered.

Autocratic men

Introduction. This section treats *autocratic persons* and focuses on personality dynamics, considering these less in terms of "badness" than in terms of personality insecurity and under-development of personality. This manner of proceeding seems more consistent with the approach in this book, and leads to the portrayal of men who are *immature* and *unmanly*.

The saying, "The buck stops here" occasionally has reasonable application, in that there are certain circumstances where a given person or a person holding a given office has to take responsibility, to take decisions – and certain circumstances where others need to fall in line with those decisions. This observation is true of particular circumstances in everyday family life and in organisations. In some organisations – such as Armed Services – this line of decisive action may be more prevalent, and more prevalent in actual combat situations. Such action may simply mark the necessary "taking of responsibility".

In speaking of the autocratic personality, I do not refer to responsible action that is functional to the family or the organisation or society. I refer to the personality type who imposes his decisions upon others, whether they be functional or dysfunctional to personal welfare, organisational welfare, or social welfare. In a colloquialism, I refer to "control freaks", "power-centred persons", or "dictators", whether minor or major.

The power-centred personality. The "power-centred personality" is usually represented as male. This may involve a failure of perception. Certainly one encounters "power-centred females" who operate mainly on the male typification. Probably the more pertinent issue is that there tend to be distinct gender differences in the way that the "power-centred personality" exercises domination. Since this book addresses guys, I simply in principle note the differences between the sexes without exploring them, and proceed to speak of the "power-centred person" in masculine terms.

For autocratic men, their "masculinity" is usually rather narrowly conceived, showing little evidence of psychosexual maturity. Masculinity is cast in crudely "macho" terms, and a "tough guy" image projected, with a fear of any semblance of weakness or softness or anything suggesting "femininity". Sex-roles for autocrats tend to be dichotomous, and any ambiguity in this area is shunned.

This kind of personality – and the traits that lead to hardening of this kind of personality – present a "problem" from the perspective presented in this book. This is because the autocrat is generally not amenable to "personality development", and typically is resistant to maturation processes that lead to *manly maturity*. This chapter section thus more focuses upon depiction of the operation of the autocratic personality and the "management" of such persons – rather than on intra-psychic and inter-psychic "development". Certain traits of this change-resistant personality are now outlined.

Autocratic personality traits. There are certain behavioural characteristics that alert us to this personality type. These are now outlined.

Unqualified statement. Whether he goes on for great length, or is short and punchy, the language of autocrats tends to baldness – to unqualified statement.

Immoderate statement. Unqualified statements tend to be blunt and unsophisticated. But it is the unwarranted use of superlatives and exaggerations that characterise the language of autocrats – their language tends to be immoderate.

Restricted emotional expression. The emotional

expressions of autocrats generally show a lack of depth and also tend to be diffuse and lack adequate specification.

Diminished affectionate and individuated personal relations. The autocratic person adopts a role identification and relates with people in terms that he sees as serving his dominating role. Personal affection and personal rather than functional and self-serving relations are generally absent. When a person ceases to serve the cause of the autocrat, he is discarded without emotional angst. Over time, the autocrat becomes more remote and handles people "administratively" and at-distance through apparatchiks.

Absoluteness of emphasis. Autocrat can use few words or be quite rambling, but their key statements will typically have an absoluteness about them – their words tend to be diktats.

Predominant reference to extreme values. Life challenges usually occur along a continuum, and the challenge typically is to find a balance in a dichotomous situation. For autocrats, persons and issues tend to be dichotomous, "one thing or another", with little tolerance for "in between" that arises where thinking, feeling, and evaluation are extended.

Inconsistencies between general and specific behaviours. The simplistic mind and the simplistic rhetoric of autocrats gives rise to a tendency for inconsistency between their rigid and conventional generalisations and the features of more specific behaviours. It is difficult to "tie down" the autocrat on such points, both because open questioning is rarely admitted, and because resort to confusing rhetoric is often used to cloud inconsistencies. Because autocrats are not introspective, they are untroubled by their own mental inconsistencies and by the inconsistencies between what is espoused and what is practised. If "religious", they thus can seemingly blithely maintain inconsistent religious espousal and practice.

Stereotypical language. The language of autocrats displays patterns of denial, stereotypical use of cliché, small variability in response and lack of shading, and much repetition. This amounts to stereotypical language, rather than language that is insightful or expressive of the actual situations being engaged.

Intolerance of ambiguity. There is an over-lap in these indicators, for behaviour congruent with language usage as captured in the sub-headings just given implies an intolerance of ambiguity. The world of autocrats tends to be "flat", rather than "multi-valenced", simplistic and unrefined. They seek unswerving or unambiguous allegiance. They build around themselves organisations of "Yes men", of minions who police non-conformity and questioning.

Some of the keynotes of this portrayal of the autocrat are now further examined.

Culture of intolerance. The "intolerance of ambiguity" is manifested in the inclination toward mechanical repetition of faulty hypotheses; inaccessibility to new experience; satisfaction with subjective and at the same time over-concrete and over-generalised solutions – serving to reinforce the submission to authority, authoritative authority, arbitrary authoritative authority. The culture of the authoritarian person and his micro-society or macro-society involves less originality; less intellectuality; less sensuality; less internalised and more externalised norms; more constricted and conformist behaviour; more conservative standards; more ethnocentric perspectives; and, of course, less personal and social independence. All these characteristics contribute to a culture of intolerance of cognitive ambiguity or emotional ambivalence. To the autocrat, ambivalence spells insecurity and provokes his movement to closure – to forced closure.

Projection of primitive internal drives. Such a depiction of the autocrat may well surprise most autocrats, or they would regard such behaviour as simply "necessary". Autocrats are pragmatists, not idealists. The autocratic personality is not introspective, and is marked by a discrepancy between conscious self-perception and the actual dynamics of conduct as seen by a detached observer. The greater the discrepancy, the more we may expect actual mal-adjustments, insecurity, self-deception, and projection. These are manifestations of arrested personality development that reflect irrational, archaic, and primitive psychic influences. These personality traits urge the autocrat to seek to impose himself on others by the use of coercive measures. The autocratic personality does not act from open, exploratory, and bottom-up psychic processes. Rather, he extroverts his own psychic state – particularly his affective psychic state – in a top-down manner.

The autocratic personality may reflect the "external world" at the point of his ascent to "leadership" – such as a situation of organisational failure or a situation of social conflict that is not amenable to compromise. But, once in "leadership", the "internal world" of the autocrat and the rhythms of his personality system become the main drivers. These drivers are primitive, and the authoritarian personality is generally psychologically immature.

These intra-psychic drivers persist when the need for directive decision-taking roles has past – that is the reason why autocrats are so driven to avert their displacement when the circumstances that gave rise to their ascent are no longer present. Unpackaging the causal influences of this behaviour would probably lead toward a Freudian perspective and unhappy childhoods such as proposed by Frenkel-Brunswik in explaining the aggression, rigidity, cruelty, superstition, externalisation and projectivity, denial of weakness, and power-orientation that she identifies in the authoritarian personality.

Need externally to police autocrats. The strong internal drive of the authoritarian personality is, however, not governed by the "objective values" of convictions that form "conscience". The "values" of the authoritarian person are highly selective and arbitrary and integrate with an egotistical world-view. In brief, their adoption is to serve the interests of the autocrat and to reinforce his *ego* – in the sense of both the "operational area of the personality" and in the egotistical sense of "egotist". It is thus difficult to make *moral* appeal to the authoritarian personality. The rhetoric of morality may be used by such people, but not the substance of morality. Essentially, the authoritarian person is a coarse person, and the appeal needs to have a certain coarseness – of the "*Do this, or else!*" kind.

While the mentality of the authoritarian personality is

coarse and primitive, skills of manipulation, deceit and of cunning have been worked over and worked over. The capacity of not-very-bright people of this kind of personality for subtle cunning is great, and averting their authoritarian behaviour calls upon close observational and surveillance skills.

The instinct to cunning in the autocrat may be enhanced where the surrounding culture or the culture of those who review actions would lead to individual and social censoring of autocratic behaviour. The prospect of being censured reinforces the tendency to disguise and transform the real motivations in order to avoid censoring and penalties. Such deception is not only of others – there also may be self-deception, as explored in the chapter on Moral Psychology. The capacity for self-deception in the authoritarian personality is enhanced by their characteristic lack of introspectiveness.

These autocratic processes of deception may be woven into some pseudo-integrity "protocol" in the execution of their deceit. This last method of deceit may often be observed as a means of "massaging" essentially illicit practices. Autocrats may make severe apparent recourse to "the law", but in a manner of pretext, not of substance. Due juridical process is alien to the mind of the autocrat. The autocrat seeks not justice, but judgement.

Archaic nature of autocratic rule. The inherent incapacity for moderation – other than short-term self-serving compromise – means that negotiated outcomes with authoritarian personalities can rarely be sustained. Reversion to black-and-white solutions, premature closure, and unqualified and unambiguous solutions will again assert themselves. Moreover, the authoritarian personality is generally quick to recognise challenge – whether covert or overt – to his dominance, and will systematically work to marginalise persons who might be instrumental in changes toward adopting more objective norms and promoting more participative arrangements (whether in the family; the firm; or in the tribe or nation). The autocratic personality is equipped to gain control in certain situations, but is not equipped with flexibility to lead to new situations. The autocratic person thus becomes archaic, and presides over increasingly archaic social systems that reflect and preserve the earlier and now archaic circumstances of his ascent to power.

Difficulty of transition from autocracy. A particular difficulty in addressing the social and emotional outlook of the autocratic person is that he is located in a particular social setting upon which he has projected his personality – whether it be a family, an organisation, or a larger society (such as a tribe or a nation). Typically, the social conditions for change will be weakly present. A family that has lived under a "dictator" is likely ill-equipped for less-coercive family life; a firm that has been run by a "dictator" is likely ill-equipped organisationally to reconstruct to a more viable social form; a nation that has been run by a "dictator" will have weak institutions of state and weak civic understandings among its citizens that ill-equip the formation of more voluntaristic and participative social and political arrangements.

Implications for psychological response. It is strange that anyone should *want* to be an autocrat, for it is not a choice for happiness – either for the autocrat or for those whom he dominates. Rarely does one see an autocrat smile – if it is not a leer, it is a cosmetic smile. The choice for autocracy is not a happy one, but then it typically is a "choice" enacted through primitive and unexamined drives, rather than through choice for human flourishment.

The implication from this discussion is that the hardened dictatorial personality is not amenable to change or to personality development. It follows that change in the surrounding culture – whether micro-culture or macro-culture – involves difficult transitions. This implies that any scope for "managing" autocrats calls for external means – not persuasion, but penalties and sanctions.

Where this leads to eventual displacement, this implies the need for strategic and integrated approaches to personal and institutional development in a post-autocrat era. At the micro-level this involves social workers and/ or community enablers; at organisational levels this requires articulation of new leadership and new decision styles; at national levels this requires what is now usually termed "nation building".

At all these levels, this is a complex task, because it can easily tilt to a different form of "autocracy" of a paternalistic kind – whether from a *"We know better"* professional condescension, or from a *"This is **the** model"* as conceived by a new dominant and assertive and often foreign culture.

Cowardly men

Deceptive appearances. Cowardliness takes many forms. Just as the "hypocrite" may be unaware of his hypocrisy because he has constructed a shield of self-deception, so also the "coward" may be unaware of his cowardice because he also has constructed a shield of self-deception. The "shield" that is most common among cowardly men may be seen where the choice is for "appearances" – for *safe* appearances – rather than a choice for a robust response to situations.

Cowardice as omission. The many forms of cowardice range across guys failing to take manly leadership in their families; guys accommodating oppression and malpractice in work places; guys failing to take manly responsibility in many and varied circumstrances. The nature of cowardice as a vice is more *omission* of action, rather than *commission* in action. As a narrative instance of this failure, I use the example of the implicit withdrawal of healthy relationship between an older man and a younger man, and the loss of mentoring that this avoidance entails. The deceptive "appearances" of course imply *social appearances* – such as how others may view or how one appears to be viewed by others or how one fears others may view one and one's relationship or relationships with a younger person or persons.

Another telling example is the guy who goes in for verbal "poofter bashing". He reveals himself as fearful that others may question his heterosexuality, and so advertises his deprecation of the feared attributes. The guy who can't speak or matters sexual or who can speak only in clinical language on matters sexual is another example. He reveals himself as fearful of "sex". A contrasting version of the cowardly behaviour is the guy who somewhat advertises his sexual exploits – usually heterosexual exploits – and who in so doing usually unknowingly advertises a lack of sexual self-confidence or at least advertises a lack of poise in self-identity (and a corollary of a lack of manly poise in moral psychology and moral behaviour).

Deceptive protocol. Yet another version of cowardliness is the undue resort to "protocol" – especially to covert protocol. By "covert protocol" I mean the interpretation of protocol that is not in the "Ethical Behaviour Manual" or is an exaggerated version of what is in the Manual, or "protocol" that is not openly acknowledged and is a kind of implicit taboo.

An example of such implicit taboos may be found in media prominence given to sexual interference by men of adolescent boys, and the consequent ascendency of perception that relationship between a man and a boy (or between a mature man and a young man) is sexually charged, and is sexually suspect – and thus is taboo. In media and in uninformed popular perception, this suspicion is often heightened where the older guy is a religious man or a cleric. Fear of this perception gives rise to the covert protocol that a man should not be together with a boy or a young man without a "chaperone" present. The absence of a chaperone is deprecated as an occasion for "scandal", and the cowardly and insecure avoid such situations and ostracise those who do not avoid such situations, who do not embrace their exaggerated covert protocols.

Stylised relationship. The effect of this attitude and performance is that healthy relations between men and boys or between older guys and young guys become stylised and attenuated. And what follows from this is that boys and young men are deprived of robust male mentoring and friendship. This of course diminishes the older guy, because he is removed from youths and the contemporary world that the youthful bring, and older guys are also removed from the satisfaction of engaging with and in seeing the maturation of young guys. But the greater loss is for boys and young men, because young guys in these circumstances are deprived of something that is crucial to the ordinary course of manly maturation – they are deprived of older male mentoring and/or of fathering. This is a terrible diminishment for male youths, and a diminishment for society. It is a diminishment that arises from a lack of manliness, from *cowardice* and from "keeping-up appearances".

Cowardly hiding behind rules, often covert rules. In so speaking, I do not deny the prudential considerations of reasonable protocol that are proper to older-male / younger-male relations (nor of course the different prudential considerations that are proper to male / female relations and of older-male / younger-female relations). Yet prudence is a reasonable quality that has a certain "balance", rather than being "absolute" or exaggerated. What I decry is the unmanly insecurity and cowardliness of men who for fear of social stricture do not realistically and naturally and wholesomely engage with boys and younger guys.

Cowardice and the psychology of social exclusion. The fearful avoidance of relationships that are contrary to unreasoned overt rules – and especially that are contrary to unreasoned *covert* rules – often amounts to cowardly behaviour that deprives younger guys of the necessary help of the society of older guys. And what I decry is the nastiness of the ostracisation that derogates those who do not observe their implicit "play safe" codes of conduct. This nastiness is seen in the covert nature of the social psychology and attendant discriminating behaviour that implicitly tries to clothe insecurity and cowardliness as virtue – that interprets cowardice as virtue rather than what it is, a *vice*.

Weak men collaborate to endow cowardice with virtue. In this scenario, the cowards become the virtuous, and the "hollow men" become the "upright men". Although the operative psychology can be personal or intra-psychic, the example applies more where the operative psychology is inter-psychic or social. That is, weak men collaborate to endow timorousness with virtue, to bolster their group identity, and to assure themselves of their "okay-ness". It is as though such men when they were boys never read the great epic classics – usually warrior epic classics – whether as books or as movies. Their psychology does not aspire to the nobility and valour of the warrior. And it is "warriors" who become leaders of men and leaders of young men and of boys. But warriors are brave, not cowardly.

Inter-psychic shields for cowardice. It is hard to make intra-psychic appeal to such men who would view valour as imprudence, and who are unmoved by "guilt" of an *omission* kind (such as what is *not done* helpfully to engage in the human development of youths). The inter-psychic nature of the ethic of such cowards acts to shield them from "shame". Their ethics are the ethics of un-contamination that are supported by inward-looking and "in-group" socialisation that reinforces their timorous and covert inter-psychic and social self-regard.

Cowardly ethics of self-deception. When such men disclose their covert ethics, it will usually only be in circumstances where the presence of a suitable set of chronies and sycophants ("Yes men") who reinforce their priggish uprightness or at least do not challenge their sham uprightness – whether "uprightness" of a political kind, a religious kind, or of a class kind. In such social settings, collaboration becomes conspiracy against those who threaten their complacency and/or their supposed respectability. To such persons and their collaborators, the ascription of "conspiracy" would provoke "shock", "horror" – because their ethics are ones of self-deception, as well as the supposed deception of their audiences.

Empowering warriors. Such persons or groups of persons have heavily invested in cultivating these psychological defences, and these defences are difficult to penetrate. Neither guilt nor shame exerts much impact upon them. One has instead to cultivate a different social perception and a different social set to displace such cabals of cowards. This may well involve displacement, rather than replacement, as valiant younger guys decline to join the stuffy set of self-satisfied and self-preserving older guys and their naïve and insecure sycophant younger followers.

In such circumstances, it may be helpful to allow more robust young guys to voice their own perceptions of the disconnection between the espoused values and the practiced values that they encounter. This can provide a foundation for these young guys to find a language and a psychology that gives form and intra-psychic and inter-psychic impetus to the emergence of personal identities and group identities that are more visionary, more open, and more *manly*.

Men engaging in deception and moral disengagement

Deception is of course a human act, rather than a masculine act. The deception practised by guys will differ from the deception practised by gals in ways that reflect their differences in personality and their differences in moral psychology. And this is the case whether deception is of the "deceiving others" kind or the "self-deceiving" kind.

The "self-deceiving" kind more applies to those who are unreflective – those who do not tend to introversion and those whose psychic processes are more social. As was suggested in the early chapter dealing with the psychology of personality, such personality types are perhaps more represented among guys than among gals – although the generalisations nevertheless apply to both guys and gals.

Selective activation and/or disengagement of moral control. Spurious moral justifications are only one of many mechanisms impinging upon the operation of moral standards in the regulation of conduct. The labels that Bandura uses generally give a sense of other moderating or reinforcing mechanisms involved in the selective activation and disengagement of moral control: moral justification; euphemistic labelling;

tendentious advantageous comparisons; displacement of responsibility; diffusion of responsibility; disregard or distortion of consequences; dehumanisation; attribution of blame; gradualistic moral disengagement; and disengagement of self-sanctions and self-deception.

This is a long list, and this chapter is already long. The labels themselves provide salient prompts for reflection. I close with some amplifcation adapting Bandura on the last two labels of "gradualistic moral disengagement", and "disengagement of self-sanctions and self-deception".

Moral disengagement. The processes of moral disengagement will not immediately transform a considerate person into an unprincipled, callous one. Rather, the change is usually achieved through gradual diminution of self-sanctions in which people may not fully recognise the changes that are occurring. Initially, individuals are prompted to perform questionable act that they can tolerate with little self-censure. After their discomfort and self-reproof have been diminished through repeated performances, the level of reprehensibility progressively increases until eventually acts originally regarded as abhorrent can be performed without much distress through processes whereby moral bearings are diminished to the point of being lost.

Disengement of sanctions. In speaking of disengagement of self-sanctions and self-deception, Bandura makes the acute observation that the deceiving self has to be aware of what the deceived self believes in order to know how to concoct the deceptions. Different levels of awareness are sometimes proposed as another possible solution to the paradox. Sometimes the defence mechanism can be refusal to confront facts. As long as one does not know the truth, what one believes is not personally known to be false. Psychological processes can be employed whereby people avoid painful or incriminating truth, either by not taking actions that would reveal the truth or by not spelling out fully what they are doing or by avoiding explorations that would make the truth known. Implicit agreements and social arrangements are created that leave the foreseeable unforseen and the knowable unknown. Such is the nature of the psychology of deceit.

Male culture that excludes

The term "male culture" has become something of a swearword in media vocabulary in Australia and elsewhere, often meaning something "sexist" in its exlcusion of females. The swear words of the general media are typically directed to a class of person who does not have media esteem (for example, a political group generally disliked among the journalists of the press gallery). The generic group that most gets "male culture" swearing is the general group of military personnel. It is "male culture" that excludes women from combat units; "male culture" that excluded women as sub-mariners, and so forth. It is "male culture" that explains recreation leave misbehaviour by military personnel. This section closes a chapter titled "Immaturity among Men", and certainly one encounters sexist male culture that wrongly excludes, and the psychological reasons for this have been canvassed elsewhere in this book. I want here instead to take opportunity to propose psychological approaches toward understanding circumstances where the inclusion of sex in organisational selection and performance is not "sexist" *per se*, but is functional to organisational performance and functional to organisational product delivery.

The issues are complex. The complexity of sex/gender issues as these operate functionally for organisational performance and organisational product delivery are increased in many contemporary settings where technological and economic changes have shifted occupational gender lines and where organisational gender cultures are in transition. I have elsewhere touched on the need for guys to allow organisational space and organisational mobility to gals where their aptitudes meet organisational needs (and, by implication, for gals to do likewise for guys). I want now to make some observations in a contrary direction – in a direction that gives recognition to circumstances where "male culture" is not something that is out-of-date and/or unfair, but where "male culture" effectively functions to advance the organisational purpose and organisational product delivery. This, indeed, is most aptly illustrated with reference to military culture – or at least to certain functional groups within military culture.

Military examples of "non-sexist" exclusion by males. I have never been in a submarine – the most recent example of what I regard as folly where the civil arm of Australian government enforced an "anti-[sex] discrimination" policy. Indeed, my Naval experience was a single day on a RAN supply ship. The biggest impression it left upon me was, "No way could I become a mariner!" I simply could not deal psychologically with such confined spaces and such sustained physical proximity with other men. Put into this context the prospect of rubbing against female breasts in passing along narrow passage-ways and closely viewing female backsides while climbing deck ladders – not to mention shared sleeping compartments and bathrooms – and the *Could not cope!* cry would become quite amplified. That's the physicality of the example, without even raising the psychology of masculine communication such as *Fuck you, mate!* said not as a sexual remark but as a *Back off, Man!* warning.

In a contemporary Naval context the actual technology of production may less favour males than earlier eras when weapon handling was more manual than electronic. We, however, deal not simply with technical questions, but with cultural questions, and cultural questions that are "gendered" ones.

There remain domains where accepting a "gendering" of the production environment and organisation enhances the product delivery. It is in this sense that the exclusion of females (and, in different circumstances, the exclusion of males) is not "sexist" in the deprecatory sense of the term, nor "discriminatory" in the deprecative sense of the term. Such exclusion arises from physiological and psychological and inherent cultural conditions of the relevant production or activity environments.

Army direct combat forces are another example. Warriors always drew upon superior masculine strength, and simply looking at photographs of the modern warrior armed with what seems to be a massive weight of varied equipment (not just rifle and bayonet!), it seems that masculine strength and endurance are more, not less, required. But, again, the physicality is not separate from the psychological, and the ways that a force of fighting men relate with one another would suffer functional diminishment by "gender mixing". To think otherwise is simply to advance the ideology of "sexual equality" above effective organisational functioning and organisational mission. On 28 September 2011 the Australian government approved the opening-up of all frontline combat roles in the Australian Defence Force to women who meet rigorous physical entry standards. This is simply an ideological "sexual equality" position that proceeds as though female bodies operate like male bodies (that do not have a menstrual cycle) and that there are not differences in sexual psychology, especially as these apply to the male social psychology in situations such as armed combat or in a football team.

Ideology of "sexual equality" when applied across-the-board. The "sexual equality" ideology proceeds as though men and women are differentiated only in their genitals, not in their whole bodies, and that minds are compartmentalised from bodies. In this view, female psychology and male psychology are simply different cultural artefacts to be reconfigured by different enculturation. Sexual differentiation is only in reproductive differentiation. And human "reproduction" is separated as "domestic" or "private" from the "public" domains of public production organisations. From this ideological viewpoint, men and women are in respects other than their reproductive equipment simply substitutable. This ideology is surreal, and needs to be presented in its surreality.

Academic examples of "non-sexist" inclusion. Having made these observations, I should say that I worked for decades in tertiary education where most of the academic staff were males and where most of the minority female staff were "feminists". Across decades, I never had an out-and-out argument with these women on workplace equity and access. The universities in which I worked had appropriate and articulate merit-based selection and promotion policies and – apart from accommodating the "non-sexist" language requirements – simply observing reasonable professional and human conduct standards ensured that there were no "gender wars". There are organisations where these basically simple conduct requirements deliver "gender equality", and contemporary technical and economic changes tend to the expansion of such organisational adaptation.

"Male culture" is not necessarily "men behaving badly". Nevertheless, what is generally the case is not universally the case. And the point of this section is to highlight that "male culture" environments are not necessarily "men behaving badly" environments of sexual discrimination. There are environments where male physicality and male psychology act congruently for organisational effectiveness and for efficiency in product delivery. Accurate psychological assessment of sex/gender configuration of organisations needs to reckon with this reality.

These observations – perhaps controversial observations – are now followed by more clearly controversial observations in the next chapter that tackle psychological approaches to the exercise of male sexuality in its genital aspect, and the complex issue of male sexuality as manifest in same-sex attraction and behaviour.

9
Immaturity among Men: key sexual issues

Introduction

Sexual issues of course are wide-ranging, and the treatment here is selective. The first section treats the immaturity and irresponsibility of simply "consensual sex". Next, the difficult topic of sexual interest in minors is examined in terms of immaturity. Next, the complex issue of homosexuality is examined in terms of arrested sexual development, and thus of immaturity. Finally, the misunderstandings in "gay" approaches to homosexuality are unpackaged. None of these treatments will be "popular", as all challenge aspects of contemporary received understandings. All in one degree or another also draw on understandings as earlier argued in the Moral Psychology chapter.

The fuckerer

The simple English word *fuck* has assumed the character of a "swear word", with latinisms, coitus or sexual intercourse, being used in more "polite" discourse. Fucker is one who "fucks", and I have coined the term *fuckerer* for one who sees this physical act as simply an exercise of his masculinity without the attendant manly responsibilities.

The contemporary scene has heightened what is an immemorial difficulty in growing to manly maturity. In every age, a guy has needed to decide *not* to be a "stallion", not to mount every available "mare". The "availability" has certainly increased, with gals now not merely flirting, but even actively propositioning guys in a kind of fee-free prostitution. In animals, the over-riding consideration is genetic strength – and in the horse example, it is the strongest stallion who mounts the mares under his protection.

Human paternity differs vastly from animal paternity. The fundamental recognition to be made is that human paternity is vastly different from animal paternity. There is no equivalent to the complex parental mother and father nurturing. This is unique to the human species. For humans, paternity is especially integral socially as well as biologically. The complex and on-going father role makes particular demands upon the sexual instinct and fertility of the human male. Typically, he is *always fertile*, but he has licence to exercise his fertility only with readiness to integrate his sexual act with a stable and complex exercise of paternity, of *fathering*.

Certainly in a popular contemporary view, the sexual act is simply "having sex", and usually having so-called "safe sex". Although contrary to the prevalent culture, I argue that this is *un*manly! *Manliness* is not established by sexual performance of an irresponsible kind that detaches the sexual act from its inherent fertility and from its proper context of the lifestyle and responsibilities proper to a husband and a father.

The issue must be adjudged in a moral context. A full account of what I am here arguing takes us into the complex territory of reasoning examined in the chapter under the heading of Moral Maturity. In some respects "reduced form" morality may serve better, because it moves more directly. The simple and direct strictures supplied by the words "fornication" and "adultery" have somewhat lost currency, especially the first, "fornication".

A cruder but direct way of putting the proposition is for a guy to ask himself this question, "When your first son is born and you are present, do you want him to emerge through an orifice that other guys have scraped?" Again, "Do you want your children's paternity to be secure?" The answers are likely to be *Yes*. The corollary to this *Yes* is a *No* to "consensual sex" where the woman is not your wife.

In ordinary terms, you are always fertile. In ordinary terms, a condom or "the pill" insults your manhood, denying your fertility, and makes you just "a fucker". There is no moral right to "consent" where the man has not embraced the status and responsibilities of "husband" and its corollary, "father"; and the man has no moral right to "consent" where the woman has not embraced the status and responsibilities of "wife" and its corollary, "mother". Outside this moral and social context, "having sex" is just *scraping*.

Being "in love" does not alter the moral evaluation. For those who are "in love", this language may seem offensive, degrading, anger-making. But being "in love" or even simply "mutual consent" remove the moral category *rape*. They do not give moral *right* to that "consent". The moral categories *fornication* and/or *adultery* remain. Without the moral right, "having sex" may well answer physiological drives and emotional drives. But in terms that uphold the responsibility and the dignity of the human male, it is not *manly*.

Coitus and the dignity of human parenting.

Outside coitus, male ejaculation – whether spontaneous or otherwise – involves the spilling of sperm. The very term, *spermatozoa*, means "seed", and this language is rooted etymologically – and often also morally – in a misunderstanding of human physiology. The human female is not simply an incubator of the male "seed". The human "seed" that the female "incubates" in fact is a *zygote*. This beginning involves the fusion of a *spermatozoon* and an *ovum* ("egg"). In "botanical analogy", it is this *fusion* of the male cell and the female cell and consequent attachment in the womb that leads to incubation and nutrition involved in human gestation. For the human female there is an enormous dignity in *coitus*, the potential dignity and enduring responsibility of motherhood. For the human male there is an enormous dignity in *coitus*, the potential dignity and enduring responsibility of *fatherhood*.

Manliness in maturity involves affirmation and guarding of this masculine dignity. It is *un*manly to be a "rake", and *un*womanly to invite a "scraper" or a "fuckerer". Complex socialisation that builds such an understanding of manly dignity and/or reflection and one's thinking through the understanding of manly dignity provide the conditions for embracing the position just argued.

Building psychological structures that support the dignity of human parenting.

In psychological terms, this means building inter-psychic ("social") structures and/or building intra-psychic structures. Sometimes, a "short cut" route can contribute to this integration, like crudely asking, "Do you want your first-born to emerge from an orifice that other guys have scraped?", or "Do you want to be Dad to a son who never has reason to question his paternity?" These simple questions can provoke penetrating answers, and answers that reinforce *manly* behaviour in guys who might otherwise exercise their randiness and/or their emotionality in ways that essentially are unmanly.

The "Last Taboo"

Recent and contemporary Western cultures have seen and see a roll-back of public and private constraints on many areas of behaviour, including sexual behaviours, such that "anything goes" – or at least the range of "what goes" is increased. Young people can "hook-up" (that is, have casual and passing sexual encounters); persons holding civic office can publicly have a "partner" (rather than a "spouse"); unnatural unions can be legitimised (as in so-called "gay marriages"), and so forth. Expressions of distaste or of disapproval of such behaviours may be viewed as "vilification" or as taking into the public domain what is regarded as the private domain. Yet some taboos remain. Bigamy, for example, remains a civil offence in most Western cultures, even though this stricture seems contrary to the dominant operating principle (or lack of principle) governing personal sexual conduct.

One area where the "shock", "horror" of taboo not merely remains, but is heightened is sexual encounter between adults and minors. When I was young, the term "child abuse" would have mainly conveyed a sense of physical disciplinary punishment that was excessive to a degree that an adult inflicted serious physical harm on a child. Nowadays, "child abuse" is shorthand for adult conduct involving the sexual interference with children, and with "abuse" often being read as *any* sexual encounter betweem an adult and a child.

Sensitive issue of sexual induction for young persons. Such a "reading" creates its own difficulties, because it virtually means that the sexual induction of children occurs only with peers or older children inducting younger children. This manner of induction certainly presents its own hazards, as children's understandings of sexuality are usually "child understandings" and children's understandings of moral issues are usually "child understandings", and as such usually deficient understandings. Earlier cultures typically had articulated protocols for inducting children into non-child sexuality – that is, rites of initiation into adulthood or into early-adulthood. Contemporary Western cultures have somewhat of a vacuum in this regard, and this vacuum has accentuated certain behaviours such as adolescent "hooking-up" (and post-adolescent "hooking-up" behaviours and variants thereof). I do not here address the sensitive and complex issue of helpful enculturation of the physical and psychological transitions in sexual maturation. I only point out that this poverty in enculturation creates its own difficulties – difficulties that are accentuated by the mental and emotional intemperance often associated with a crude *taboo!* mentality.

Difficulties raised by fear mentality. One such difficulty is that captured by the current phrase "stranger danger", as used to foster wariness in parents and in children to sexual dangers from persons not known to them. While there are certainly dramatic and traumatic examples of such "stranger danger", this language nevertheless conceals the fact that most sexual abuse of children is *not* from strangers, but from persons known to the child. Indeed, the dominant pattern of sexual abuse is within families. And the dominant incidence of sexual interference of children is by *males* – and especially from non-paternal males. Understanding why this is so is rather complex, and it will not be unpackaged here. What I wish in a limited way here to examine is the immaturity and the immorality of such sexual interference, adopting a psychological approach in this examining.

The functional roles of social and psychological inhibitions. While recognising that the blunt mental and emotional nature of taboos involves its own dangers, I nevertheless close this section by showing how this "last taboo" should act as a cue for the retrieval of other taboos – for the recognition that some taboos may serve social and psychological functions that inhibit dysfunctional human behaviours.

The dominant cue in understanding adult sexual interference with children is "immaturity". Essentially, we encounter guys (it is mainly guys who are the offenders, and, moreover, this book is mainly addressed to guys) whose maturity in psychological terms does not match their age and physiological maturation. That is, we encounter guys who in terms of psycho-sexual development are not "adult" – or at least in the mode in which the sexual interference occurs are not "adult".

Mature sexual fantasy. Typically, sexual arousal involves "fantasy". I do not use the term in a sense that necessarily involves deprecation. For example, imagining and/or actually encountering female breasts is a typical trigger in sexual arousal among guys. One sees this at work in the strength of desire among young guys pictorially to view female breasts as part of the building of their sexual imagination (the psychic construction of sexual fantasy), and the differential building of their own sexuality focusing on the penis.

Immature sexual fantasy. Where one encounters a guy whose sexual arousal is prompted by the sexually immature (that is, by a child or youth), one encounters a guy who is operating from non-adult sexual fantasy. This may occur in cases of episodic psycho-sexual regression (as where a father transfers his sexual fantasy from his wife to his daughter), or in cases where stable psycho-sexual maturation has not been achieved.

"Children in men's bodies". Speaking of guys, I call such people, "Children in men's bodies". That is, we deal with guys whose sexual fantasies are those of a child or a youth, and who enact the sexual games of children or youths. Or at least enact the sexual games of children or youths who are not psychologically constrained by taboos (such as bigger brother should not touch erotic areas of little sister) or not constrained by social policing of taboos.

From children's games to adult acting.
When I say "children's games" I do not imply that children or youths are perverts. Rather, I imply that child and youth exploratory activity is typically of a "game" kind and that children and youths have a curiosity about their own sexuality and the sexuality of others that may be enacted in games. The "game" aspect of sexuality remains present in adult sexuality, but not as the dominant aspect. Instead, sexuality in the adult person becomes purposive and becomes evaluated in a purposeful field – that is, it becomes *moral* activity.

The world of the child has purpose, and in certain measure games operate purposefully in child and youth development. But games for children and youths importantly remain but *games*, and are not conducted in a world of responsibility. They tend to be conducted in a world of "amusement" or of "fun" or of "exploration" and "curiosity". Children tend to be indulgent. It is the *parent* who cries, "Enough!" or "Be careful!" Children wish to take treats when they want treats; adults police the taking of treats so that due time and moderation are observed.

Psychological immaturity and age-inappropriate enaction. When I say "A child in a man's body", I mean an adult guy who psychologically is like a child – a guy who in significant respects embraces self-gratification and has personal habits of unrestrained self-gratification. Where the deficiency in human development is marked in the area of psycho-sexual development, one encounters a guy who embraces or episodically reverts to self-gratification that in psychological terms is age-inappropriate.

Danger of habitual child self-indulgence in adults. It would be very wrong to see obese men as "child abusers" or as "perverts". But when one encounters obese people (whether male or female), one encounters people who typically lack restraint in eating. Of course some people are more disposed to put on weight than others, and thus some people need more than others to exercise restraint in eating habits. But one only gets obese by eating more than one's nutritional requirements. And one only eats more than one's nutritional requirements when over time one has not learned accordingly to moderate one's eating habits.

This is a metaphor for the "Man in a child's body" language. But only partly a metaphor. I remember being shocked during a visit to the largest prison in Australia holding mainly men who were (are) child sex offenders, and being astonished to see there a young man who was exceedingly good looking and with a fine physique. Why astonished? Because I had not previously encountered a child sex offender whose childish indulgence of himself did not also extend to his overall physiognomy as seen in an ugly obesity.

Necessity in the maturation process of habituating restraint. Underscoring habituating restraint in the maturation process is a generalisation, and – like all generalisations – may be mis-used. But it conveys the sense that "maturity" involves the exercise of *restraint*, and not merely the "exercise of restraint", but the "*habituation* of restraint". That is, speaking again in the metaphor of psycho-sexual development, one deals with a process of psychological habituation such that one's world of sexual fantasy becomes one of *adult* sexual fantasy, not of *child* sexual fantasy.

Persons who have made this psychological transition are simply not sexually drawn to or aroused by children. A guy who on entering a room encounters a four-year-old raising her dress and looking flirtingly at him will simply not respond. If he is ill at ease, he may be flustered; if he is more experienced, he will know how to divert such behaviour; if he is "a child in a man's body" he may be aroused to provoke such signals and/or inappropriately respond to such signals.

Moral language reflects age and responsibility. The term "inappropriate" is soft language that leads into the moral psychology involved in such matters. When speaking in a corrective manner with children we most often will use the term "silly" ("Don't be *silly!*") or else "naughty" ("That's *naughty!*"). Especially with small children we will rarely use the term "wicked" ("*Wicked* boy!"), since this implies both a gravity of action *and* an intentionality that we usually cannot attribute to a child, especially to a small child. When an adult does something that is "silly", we are more likely to use terms such as "irresponsible" or "foolish", and when "naughty" to use a term such as "childish". But when an adult enacts something that in and of itself is damaging and especially gravely damaging, we will think of the term "wicked", even though this may be translated in fashionable language to some more neutral term.

Moral capability and exercise of responsibility viewed as learned and constructed psychological competences.

Typically, people will be willing to use the term "wicked" when dealing with enactment of sexual interference with children. In which case, people invoke a severe moral judgement on the act and on the responsibility of the adult actor. In so doing, people impute an adult capability and responsibility to adjudge the harm of actions and the morality of actions – in this case, actions of sexual interference with a child. But both the moral capability and the exercise of responsibility are *learned* and/or *constructed* psychological competences. Adults who psychologically are but children do not have these faculties and/or these competencies.

This lack does not *excuse*, but it does *explain*. It *explains* why there is such a tendency to recitivitism among child sex offenders – because we deal with men whose moral psychological development has not progressed to an adult poise. Sometimes this may be due to circumstances, such as social circumstances that are not conducive to human maturation or that retard human maturation. But more often the dominating circumstance has been and is *choice* for behaviour that in a young person is *child-like* and in an emerging adult and in an adult is *self-indulgent*. This self-indulgence focuses on enacting what pleases or amuses or gratifies the adult, and that regards another as but an object for one's pleasure, amusement, or gratification. That is, the child or young person who is the subject of sexual interference is treated as an *object* – as an object of sexual pleasure, amusement, or gratification.

Rights of children and youths to their state of life (as child or as youth) must be upheld. The rights of a child or youth are to the state of a child or youth. These rights are to receive nurture, including maturing nurture and the right to respect for human dignity. Where these inherent rights are subjugated to the indulgence of the "child" within the "adult" – subjugated to the *wicked* child within the adult – we encounter sexual abuse of the child or the youth. This bent toward indulgence may be constrained by external circumstances provided by behaviour protocols (such as "Never be alone with a child") and taboos (such as "Do not speak with a minor on matters sexual"). But such constraints do not remedy the bent toward such indulgence. Indeed, in the case of adults of normal maturity, such constraints and taboos may even act dysfunctionally for healthy nurturing in normal adult-child relationships.

Dealing with persons with incapacity for psycho-sexual reconstruction. In respect of adults who are but "children in adult bodies", such protocols and taboos do not change the underlying condition. Changing the underlying condition involves the reconstruction of the person, or the psychological reconstruction of the person. This construction and reconstruction is in terms that are at once intra-psychic, inter-psychic, and psycho-sexual. The capacity for that reconstruction may not be adequate to the task.

As an analogy, we may notice that it is relatively easy for a child to learn a second language, and relatively difficult for an adult to learn a second language – and some adults may manifest an incapacity to learn a second language. The fact is that, generally speaking, certain psychological constructions occur at certain ages (at certain life-eras), and if they are not learned in those eras they may *never be learned*. The "spoilt child" may as an adult remain a "spoilt child". The child whose psycho-sexual development has been arrested or has suffered trauma may as an adult retain that child psycho-sexual state and other psychic states that are child-states.

Motivational aspects. Moreover, at any life era the learning capacity is integrally related to the learning *motivation*. The person who *wants* to live a self-indulgent life is unlikely to engage the psychological construction of responsible adulthood. The person who *wants* to live a self-indulgent life is unlikely to invest in the processes of constructing moral reasonings or in the processes of strengthening adherence to the practice of moral reasonings. Quite simply, such a person lacks *character* in a moral sense.

An adult person who has not developed character is *incapable* of habitually acting with moral poise. One does not "grow" *character* in the same way as one "grows" in physicality. Physically, one can become adult without becoming an adult *morally*. Setting aside those who are mentally deficient, we typically attribute *moral responsibility* for such moral irresponsibility.

Necessity of external constraint of persons who lack intra-psychic resources. Experience and prudence teaches us that such ingrained moral irresponsibility often is weakly subject to remedy. And this is so because "remedy" involves a major psychological reconstruction of the person – where the person is unlikely either deeply to *want* to undertake and/ or unlikely in his present life-era to have the capacity to undertake such psychic reconstruction. He may be a "damaged person", but often it will be safer to say that he is a "vicious person". Persons who so lack the intra-psychic resources to deal with perversity or with latent perversity are persons whose lives need to be governed by protocols and/or by policing and/or by imprisonment and punishment.

Implications for a project of moral psychological development for children and youths. The above sounds fatalist. The non-fatalist implication is that the project of moral psychological development is a serious and necessary project among the young. It is integral to education in the widest sense. And it is essential that this educational culture not be frightened of matters sexual and should be able to deal morally with matters sexual. This educational enculturation should deal in a manner that – while acting with prudence and in an age-appropriate manner – avoids secrecy and contributes to the emergence of robust sexual identity. Such sexual enculturation should not be prudish and should cultivate a moral sense and fearlessness in sexual identity and in fitting sexual behaviour.

"Sex" should not be treated as a *taboo* topic. In important respects this education, while always reinforcing sexual complementarity, is probably best mainly addressed in single-sex terms; that is, men to boys and women to girls. The "moral of the story" is that "sex" should *not* be a taboo topic in dealing with children. But "sex" in the culture of child education should be "age-appropriate", and allow graduated sex-education that matches where the child's curiosity is heading.

And "sex" in the culture of child education should be "relational", building a sense of sex as primarily ordered to family life and to responsible procreation.

Such a project is a big "call" in a context where the "adult" world often sees sex quite otherwise (What is conjured by the terms "Adult bookstore" or "Adult [sex] shop" or "Adult website"?), and where media such as "girls' magazines" portrays sex in quite different terms – as but "fun" or as but manipulation of boys, as in the current term "toy boy". Failure to address this "tough agenda" sets up a new generation of sexual exploiters and of the sexually exploited.

Weak formation backgrounds of clerical child/youth sex offenders. The sexual abuses that have most attracted publicity have been those of a small proportion of religious or clerical men. The public examination of their offending has generally involved little recognition of the inappropriate early-age institutionalisation that so often was the case for these offenders and that contributed to the arresting of their psycho-sexual development. With the later wave of such offenders an added significance was weak moral formation – weaknesses in moral psychology both in (1) the cognitive terms of philosophy; in (2) personal or intra-psychic terms; or in (3) social or inter-psychic terms.

Need to engage realistic human development for building robust psycho-sexual identity. Contemporary failures to address this "tough agenda" means a new generation of guys who will be undeveloped in moral psychology and undeveloped in psycho-sexual maturity. This task in psychological development is hazardous, but it has to be engaged. This engagement in certain respects is "personal" in the intra-psychic sense. But mainly it is inter-psychic or "social", since it involves the development of social identity – the social psychological development of identity, including the social psycho-sexual development of identity.

A cultural environment that places undue emphasis on protocol actually acts dysfunctionally for this human development, and cultivates a "safe" mentality rather than a "robust" mentality. Whether recognised or not, this approach cultivates the counsel of St Jerome in matters sexual: *flee!* Where this is combined with an unduly syllogistic and cerebral philosophical treatment of morality, including sexual morality, this "contemporary" approach amounts to another form for arresting integral human development, including arresting of psycho-sexual development. In this scenario there may be recourse to the *language* of "human development" in articulation and in curriculum. But the *practice* may be more to cultivate guys who are *not* manly, and who lack ease and self-confidence in their sexuality. Under the more "modern" programs, both *guilt* (the intra-psychic restraint) and *shame* (the inter-psychic restraint) may be cultivated to operate, but at the cost of manly physical and psychological vigour.

Homosexuality as sexual immaturity

From ideology to psychological understanding. In contemporary ideology, at least that popularised in the media, this heading will be a "red flag", and perhaps enrage. I do not have an intention to enrage. Nor do I have an intention to stigmatise. My intention is to move away from ideology and move toward understanding, toward psychological understanding. Further, at this point I am not treating "immaturity" in a generalised sense as in "He's an immature person." I am addressing only *an aspect* of sexual maturation.

Some insights from Freud. As this book unfolds, the ramified senses in which I use the term "maturity" unfold. Before researching for this book, I had only read "about" Freud's psychology, and in reading Sigmund Freud for himself (albeit, partial reading only and in translation) the obverse "*im*maturity" took new pointedness. Freud's psychology mainly reflects his clinical experience, which is mainly with neurotics. And it mainly deals with intra-psychic processes, or at least examines and addresses psychological issues in mainly intra-psychic terms. Further, his psychological approach with neurotics gives significance to influences that are *not* in the consciousness of his subjects – gives significance to the psychology of the "sub-conscious" in its different strata. In this, Freud often locates the genesis of neuroses in eras of life that have slipped from consciousness or have been repressed from consciousness – particularly eras of life that pre-date language fluency and/or involving trauma or involve failure of psychic resolution.

Freudian psycho-sexual stages. Freud divides life eras into three encompassing periods: (1) infancy; (2) a childhood stage of "latency" (better, of *relative* latency); and (3) the long and composite era running from adolescence to emerging adulthood and extending throughout adulthood. The most distinctive era of Freud's analysis is the earliest – infancy – with this infancy era typified in a threefold metaphor.

The metaphor for the earliest is that of breast nurture: sucking, the "*oral* stage". The second is that during which the child is conscious of bowel evacuation but is not yet toilet trained: the "*anal* stage". The third of these early eras focuses on the penis: the "*penile* stage". In respect of this last stage, Freud has been the subject of vigorous feminist critique that sees him as "sexist", because he applies the penile metaphor also to female subjects for the last era before moving from infancy to childhood. The feminist critique of this aspect of Freud's psychology may well have some validity – but the interests investigated in this book are in psychological approaches to male maturation, and this allows me to sidestep this contention.

In speaking of the infancy era, Freud speaks of infant "oral sexuality"; infant "anal sexuality"; and infant "penile sexuality". His use in this context of the term "sexuality" made more sense to me when read as "infant sensuousness". This simple change in language allows one to connect with much "adult" sensuousness that involves the eroticisation of what is not erotic in a genital sense of "sexual" – for example, the hersuit or hairy male chest may be eroticised such as is seen in the way that it may be seen as daring for a guy to discard a necktie and to have his shirt somewhat unbuttoned.

In coming to terms with Freud's typification of sexual / sensual, I was assisted by a flash-back memory as a boy of seeing a baby boy suddenly looking so happy with himself and gurgling happily – and my asking his mother, "Why is he so happy?" Only many decades later after reading Freud did I make sense of the mother's reply, "He just pooped himself!" This memory made sense for me of Freud's "anal stage" as a sexual or sensual metaphor.

Freud on arresting or regression in psycho-sexual identity. This identification of anal pleasure led to another memory – a recall of what in "gay" culture is termed "rimming"; that is, the licking by one guy of the anal area of another guy. Investigating this led me to research some internet "gay" video pornography. As it happens, the first clip that I encountered involved a guy sticking his thumb in the mouth of another guy while heading for his arse with tongue penetration of the anus. The sucking / sucked subject meanwhile occupied himself with much groaning of a "keep this up!" kind. This and several other such contemporary video clips reinforced for me Freud's thesis about pre-conscious sensual "oral", "anal", and "penile" stages that later may take erotic signification. This "research" also reinforced for me Freud's thesis of homosexuality as arrested and/or regressive sexual "development".

The direction in the third of Freud's overall life eras – the one running from adolescence – focuses on *relational* sexuality; that is, focuses on [heterosexual] coitus. The direction in the first of Freud's overall life eras – the infancy era – focuses on *self.* That is, infant sexuality/sensuality is viewed as auto-eroticism. And homosexuality is viewed by Freud as essentially auto-erotic – as involving same-sex sexual encounter that is mutual self-pleasuring rather than substantively relational. Of course, "heterosexual" encounter can similarly be but mutual auto-eroticism – as some viewing of "straight" video pornography would quickly verify.

For Freud an adult auto-erotic focus of sexual encounter on primitive oral/anal/penile pleasuring is viewed as *regressive* in nature – as diverting sexual encounter from adult heterosexual expression that is substantively relational. In my reading (which is not a complete reading), Freud does not proceed to construct a moral psychology that would link the relational quality of heterosexual encounter with an ontology of procreation. Freud's psychology focuses on the psychology of neurosis in terms of intra-psychic dysfunction. He thus identifies a dominating homosexuality as psychological dysfunction that arrests subjects in a pre-mature psycho-sexual era and/or that involves subjects in psychic regression to pre-mature psycho-sexual eras. Thus, in Freudian terms, homosexuality manifests an arrested and/or a regressive psycho-sexual state.

Inhibition and normal psycho-sexual development. There is a certain inaccuracy in my last sentence, in so far as Freud recognises that the normal person (that is, the non-neurotic person) encounters *all* the stages of psycho-sexual development, and in some measure *retains* all the stages of psycho-sexual development. That is, in some measure *all* persons have an inclination to auto-eroticism, and in some measure *all* persons have an inclination to homosexual expression of sexuality. But most persons in one degree or another inhibit their auto-erotic tendencies and their homo-erotic tendencies. Where this inhibition is rooted in trauma, it becomes a cue for later neuroticism, psycho-sexual neuroticism. This neuroticism may not be understood by the subject, especially where rooted in pre-conscious or pre-language life eras – and thus necessarily located in the sub-conscious mind.

In most subjects, however, the inhibition is located in *normal* early socialisation of the *"Don't suck your thumb"* kind, or the toilet training of *"Dirty"* / *"Wash your hands"* kind. Thus for most people, the thumb ceases to be a source of oral sensuousness and erotic satisfaction, and the anus likewise. Indeed, since foecal matter is a prime transmitter of infection, it is hard to see that "rimming" does not expose the "rimmer" to grave health risk. From a physician viewpoint, the inhibitions surrounding anal pleasuring will be "normal". From a Freudian psychological viewpoint, the inhibitions surrounding anal pleasuring will be "normal". The "normal guy" will regard a good shit with a well-formed and pliable stool as not unpleasurable, but not as something that in and of itself is sought, and not something to be prolonged.

Withdrawal of inhibition in psycho-sexual regression. By contrast, the characteristic of video pornography, whether "gay" / "lesbian" or otherwise, is the *prolongation* of sensual pleasure, including of kinky erotic pleasure. The fucking seems to go on interminably, the licking and the groaning seems to go on interminably, and the guys seem to have to work so hard to bring themselves to ejaculation and the noises accompanying ejaculation seem remarkable. In short, the sustained action seems to be obsessive to the point of being *boring*. Surely, there are other things to do with one's time than to keep up all this excitation of sexual or sexualised senses rather than getting on with some other life activities! Whether "gay" /"lesbian" or otherwise, the kind of sexual performance presented in video pornography seems obsessive and degrading and regressive. In the words of the major section heading, such performances seem immature – indeed, *are* immature.

But there is a point to be further underscored in a Freudian approach to this psychology of sexuality. And this is the point that such tendencies are *present* in the typical person, but that the psychological development of the typical person involves psychic construction that activates inhibitions about certain sexual expressions and activity – and instead directs sexual expression and activity in directions that have social psychological approbation. That is, a Freudian perspective recognises the possible presence of elements of "homosexuality" in the psycho-sexuality of the typical person, but recognises also that expression of homosexuality will be restrained in the typical person. That is, the typical person may in his psycho-sexual nature have in varying measure a strain of homosexuality. But this strain does not make him "homosexual" or even "latently homosexual" in the common usage of those terms.

Homosexuality does not in itself make a repressed "gay". Further, to use the jargon of the recent period, such elements of homosexuality do not thereby make the typical person a repressed "gay" who needs to "come out" and to achieve "sexual liberation". This term, "gay", has gained currency with those who wish to promote an overt homosexual lifestyle, a public acting-out of homosexuality, as a sexuality having public approbation. I do not accept this seeking for public approbation.

A case against public approbation in terms of moral psychology can of course be argued. A case in terms of social order can of course be argued. But Freudian psychology is not substantively moral psychology or social psychology, but the psychology of neuroticism and the psychology of non-neuroticism or of normalcy – both in mainly intra-psychic terms. The "gay" understanding of psychology is not sustainable in the terms that I have just argued – whether these be intra-psychic, moral psychology, or social psychology. As I view it, the "gay" position is predicated on mis-understanding.

Homosexuals are not "sick". Having said this, it is also essential to say that a response of violence toward homosexual persons or response that creates emotional trauma for homosexual persons is firmly to be avoided. The person with homo-erotic tendencies is not to be regarded as "sick" or as a social menace, and pressure for "sexual re-orientation" would likely be dysfunctional socially and psychically. Persons of homo-erotic inclination can live "normal" lives and function as "normal" members of society. I shall reinforce this point later, and at this point simply underscore this social and psychological fact that homosexual persons can lead normal lives, both personally and socially. This does not imply support – either explicit or implicit – for "gay" lifestyles. The mis-understandings on which the "gay lifestyle" is predicated are now further examined.

The "gay" mis-understanding

This mis-understanding could involve a whole book, and not a portion of a book chapter. Perhaps the cornerstone of the "gay" mis-understanding is the same as the cornerstone of the heterosexual "partner" mis-understanding. This is that the character of sexual lifestyle is particular to the person or to the persons concerned – and not to be dictated by others or by society. Further, the sexual lifestyle of the persons concerned should according to their wishes be granted public recognition, even approbation. Thus, the "right" to "gay marriage", and thus the "right" to property settlements on the separation of partnering arrangement – with property settlements analogous to those applying to civil heterosexual divorce seen as a social "right".

Mis-conceived notion of "gay rights". The first cornerstone of the those heralding a "gay" position is the claiming a "right" publicly and sexually to define themselves as they please, and not according to how others please – how "society" pleases, or the majority "society" pleases. The second cornerstone is of a *"That's the way I am"* kind or a *"That's the way I've always been"* kind. These claims are now considered.

Mis-conceived notion of homosexual genesis. From the second cornerstone, the subjects may claim that they did not choose their sexual orientation. They claim not simply their "coming out", but that the public assertion of homosexual identity and homosexual behaviour is simply an expression of who they are in some determinative *"The way I am"* sense. That is, they see their "gay-ness" as inherent, and not as socially constructed and/or as psychologically constructed. This I think over-simplifies the complexities of the issues and the psychological and psycho-social complexities of "choice".

Some of this complexity may be alluded to in commonplace terms by two pointed examples. First, and speaking in respect of males, every boy goes through a period of sexual interest in his own sex. The second commonplace pointed example is the evidence that "gay" subjects rarely will report satisfactory mentoring relationships with their father or with a mature male mentor with a secure heterosexual identity.

"Normalcy" of a period of same-sex interest. The first example does not imply that every boy goes through a period of "homosexuality". Rather, every boy goes through a period or through periods when in psychological and social terms he is establishing his sexual identity with reference to his *own sex* – that is, with reference to other males. This period or periods of same-sex sexual identification among boys and young men will still be applicable while girls and young women will have shifted to working at their sexual identification with an enhanced focus on the *other sex*. That is, girls in physical and psycho-sexual terms normally manifest an emergence of heterosexuality earlier than boys – typically, about two years earlier. During this period when girls are ahead of boys in this sexual identity aspect, boys may "hate" girls and prefer boy-only company. The "gay" subject who remembers himself as *"Always that way"* remembers himself in that psycho-sexual era, but – unlike his heterosexual peers – has not made or has weakly made the identity transition from that life era.

"Normalcy" of same-sex mentoring in transfer to other-sex interest. The second commonplace pointed example takes up the evidence that "gay" subjects rarely will report satisfactory mentoring relationships with their father or with a mature male mentor with a secure heterosexual identity. That is, from a psychological viewpoint, "gay" subjects typically have not benefited from a close male role model or close male society that has reinforced the psycho-sexual transition that occurs in moving from the era of relative sexual latency to the eras during which masculine heterosexual identity is more actively constructed psychologically. At crucial life eras, the "gay" subject typically exemplifies the effects of "under-fathering" and/or of "mis-fathering".

By under-fathering, I refer to neglect in the father-son relationship, whether by the absence of a father or of a credible father figure or father figures, or a distancing that arises from psychological incompatibility between father and son (such as occurs where the boy is "sensitive" or "artistic" and the father is neither, or *vice-versa*). By mis-fathering, I refer to where the father or father figures by their behaviour have mishandled the boy – such as being too harsh or having unrealistic expectations of the boy, or by using the boy as an object of sexual gratification, or habitually diminishing the boy's self-esteem.

In normal psycho-sexual development, a boy or a young man is hugely handicapped where he does not have a credible and trusted male mentor father or father figure. Boys and young men build psychologically their masculine identity in important respects with reference to their peers. But they build psychologically – and also physically – their emerging adult masculine identity with reference to a father figure or father figures, with reference to a man or men whom they wish to emulate. A boy or young man without a man whom he wishes to emulate is a boy or a young man who is handicapped in his construction of his heterosexual masculine identity.

Psycho-sexual identity deficiencies to some extent remediable. Such "boys" are prominent in the biographies of "gay" men. And these "gay" men typically do not make the connection that such identity deficiencies may be remediable. That is, a "boy" can be late in finding a confident manhood. In much the same way as a gap in a boy's learning in an educational curriculum sense often can later be remedied, so, too, a gap in a boy's sexual transition to manhood may be remedied. In much the same as the educational remedy may involve going to "night school", such as a TAFE adult education program, the remedy in the psycho-sexual development of a "boy" may involve a decision to *"Do something!"*. That is, the remedy involves *choice*.

The "choice" may not bring the subject to a late-found heterosexuality. It is often the case that the early and not-conscious psycho-sexual construction prevails. Thus we often should not expect a choosing *"not* to be homosexual". Rather, we should encourage a choice "not to *act out* a homosexuality". This involves a decision *not* to embrace a "gay" lifestyle, along with a decision simply to *act out* like an ordinary guy.

Choosing what we act out. The married heterosexual guy may well be bored sexually with his wife and may be drawn to extra-marital sexual fantasy. This does not mean that he therefore acts out and becomes an adulterer. Likewise, the guy who is drawn to homo-erotic fantasy does not therefore become a sodomite and pursue a route of sexual exploits that lead to all sorts of debased sexual acts. As I argued in an earlier section, the guy whose sexual attraction tends to homo-eroticism may live as "normal" a life as a citizen as a "straight guy", and lead as vigorous and satisfying and productive life as any "straight guy".

My chief purpose in this section has been to portray the psycho-genesis of marked homosexual disposition, not to "demonise" that disposition, nor to portray the homosexual guy in terms as seen in "gay" video pornography. This pornography and the lifestyle segments there portrayed are those of "gay" acting-out culture. Being "homosexual" in one degree or another does not necessarily entail "gay" acting-out. That's my point in saying that persons of homosexual inclination can *act out* like ordinary guys. And in general terms, the homosexual person may be a *mature* person, not an immature person.

Adopting helpful sexual identity. The language of "not to act out" and to "act out" *sounds* dangerous, because it sounds false – "*sounds* false", not *is* false. The fact is, however, that *for every person* the adoption of an identity involves behavioural decisions of an "acting out" kind. That is, such behavioural decisions – whether consciously or otherwise – involve adopting behaviours that cast the subject in a certain social identity and where to some extent the intra-psychic identity "follows" the social psychological identity and behaviour.

In something as simple as walking in a manly style (by which I do not mean "strutting" or "swaggering"), a "boy" may unconsciously emulate a male mentor and as a "boy" may consciously cultivate a walking style in much the same way as he might cultivate sitting still rather than fidgeting. A certain kind of fidgeting may be avoided for inter-psychic reasons and a certain manner of walking may be avoided for inter-psychic reasons. The fact is that our "body language" as one form of "social representation" is in significant part cultivated in both intra-psychic and inter-psychic terms. As he shifts from boyhood to manhood, a mature guy exercises sensibilities to these social and psychological facts.

The choice and decision that I am proposing does *not* imply that the subject who is more inclined homosexually than heterosexually sets himself to date gals or to "lay" gals. Rather, it involves simply making decisions that reinforce his ease with a certain sexual identity and declining decisions that undermine the identity that he is claiming. A corollary of this decision may be his recognition – even if it be only *pro tem* recognition – that his lifestyle will not involve sexually engaging with other persons. Many a man who has not found marriage – and many a man whose marriage has failed – faces similar life decisions and enactments.

Correct conceiving of "rights". Making such sexual enactment decisions is predicated upon the recognition that sexual acting-out is not necessarily mandated, that sexual acting-out is not simply one's "right". Making such decisions calls on a certain psychological maturity that I regard as *manly maturity*. It is in stark contrast to those who promote "gay rights" and who demand to have what they *want*. Manly decisions for responsible sexual enactment and restraint involve struggle and sacrifice, but bring fruits in manly ease and peacefulness and in enhanced manly drive in life's endeavours – and even perhaps in the emergence of a belated heterosexuality.

Helpful habituation as building virtue. The tentativeness of the language "even perhaps" is intended. I am not proposing or intending an intra-psychic suppression or denial of sexual inclination. Intra-psychically this would be akin for example to denying or supressing movements of jealousy or of fear. In these examples, the better psychic response is to enact a generosity or bravery. Others may not be aware that one is "being generous" or "being brave", and one will not be deluding oneself that one's first response was generosity or bravery. One rather is aware that one's chosen enactments are more helpful to others and to oneself.

As I have earlier argued, chosen enactments that are sustained tend to habituate, and helpful habituations are rightly labelled *virtues*. This is an instance of *manly virtue*.

The succeeding chapter draws together key elements presented in earlier chapters to sketch some Overall Perspectives on *manly maturity*. This is followed by a chapter that treats applications of the psychological approaches so far developed to the mentoring of boys, youths and young men as they seek to build and to claim their own *manly maturity*.

10
Manly Maturity:
Some Overview Perspectives

Introduction: a set of characteristics

I expect that it is now evident that the descriptors "manly" and "maturity" as here employed for a psychological approach to personal maturation are in significant respects "cultural products". If I were, for example, to say, "Clean shaven, short back and sides, gym freak, knows and follows a football code ...", the picture would quickly be of a guy who in physique and personal presentation would look "fitting" in a modern Armed Services uniform. Such guys – young and not-so-young – I think look great. Yet a guy of such "looks" could also be one who falls foul of reasonable military discipline and/or more general social expectations for mature conduct.

There is a place for prescriptiveness, including the kind of prescriptiveness in disciplined service organisations. But I am not here treating the case for such "prescription". Inevitably, readers will gain glimpses – or more than glimpses – of what I "like" in "manly maturity", and what I "don't like". Yet the book is not essentially about personal "likes" and "dislikes", nor even firstly simply about "cultural products". What we think as "manly" and as "mature" will take a cultural form such as was treated in "social representations". But such a manner of expression, identification, shape, and performance may embody and communicate something more essential.

In saying "something more essential" it might be thought that I think masculine physicality determines the matter. I think that masculine physicality is a significant determinant, but not *the* determinant. In saying "something more essential" it might be thought that I think an intrinsic morality determines the matter. I think that masculine morality is a significant determinant, but not *the* determinant.

I have tried to convey that we are dealing with a *set of characteristics* that have over-lapping components. Even where one component or another has its own integral character ("ontological" character) as in masculine physicality and masculine morality, it will still find varied cultural expression in matters such as identification, shape, and performance.

As a *set* of characteristics, "manly maturity" involves variety, versatility, and complexity in its composition. Different guys may have different aspirations for their "manly maturity", and different guys in different cultures may differently identify, shape and express their "manly maturity". In this sense, what I "like" is *not prescriptive*, and different guys will differently configure their building of *manly maturity*.

Manly maturity as a work of discovery and personal identity

Why do I labour this point? It's because from the values position that I espouse and from my psychological understanding, I emphasise that "manly maturity" for each guy has to be a work of discovery, identity, expression, and social representation that is congruent with *his* person. It's not adopting "another person", "some-one-else's person", or "society's person" – or at least not simply such an adoption.

One's "manly maturity" has to be an affirmation of "who one is" *in oneself* and "who one chooses to be" for oneself and *in human society*. In psychological terms, "manly maturity" is going to be *inter*-psychic. But it has also to be *intra*-psychic.

I place emphasis on both the intra-psychic and the inter-psychic, but probably I place more emphasis on the intra-psychic. In a sense this captures the more intra-psychic value system of modern Western culture. But it also captures my espoused values in respect of the human person, and captures my espoused values of personal moral responsibility. Further, it captures the "psychological approach" as developed in this book.

Variety in the set of maturity characteristics. Right from the first chapter treating the Psychology of Personality, I have proposed that different people have different personalities, and that the different personalities are also composite sets. Right from the start, I've seen it as important that we "own" our own personality. And not "own" our personality in the sense simply of a "constant", but in a sense something like, "This is the personality that I need to use and develop and live with creatively and helpfully." One's personality is a bit like one's body. I would like a bigger-bulk body than I have. To some extent I can work at gaining bulk, and I have enjoyed doing so. But for it really to "work", I have nevertheless to work with "what I've got"; I have to take advantage of the physique that I have got; to develop that physique within the endowments that are mine, and enjoy and usefully apply the developing physique that is mine.

The psychological challenge is analogous. And the psychological challenge is not detached from the physiological one. The human person is either male or female – I'm not treating abnormality in sexual physiognomy – and the human person is thus both sexed *and* gendered. Our psychology is thus sexed *and* gendered. And that's why I've confined myself in this book to *manly maturity*.

Psychological appropriation of male physiology. A component of this manly maturity involves psychological appropriation of a male physiology and physiognomy. Not all guys have a truck-like endowment of physiognomy, not all guys are going to have a generous distribution of body hair, or a generous endowment of head hair. But all guys have male genital equipment, a greater proportion of muscle and a lesser proportion of fatty tissue than most gals, more generous and more widely distributed body hair than most gals. And, to repeat, all guys need to develop their male physique within the endowments that are theirs, and to enjoy and usefully to apply the developing physique that is theirs.

This can happen un-self-consciously. But it can also happen consciously (even if not *self*-consciously). Generally speaking, guys have more capacity than gals to develop their physique in ways that they choose. Gals can give tone and shape to their bodies through exercise and lifestyle choices. But guys are more able to choose their body development, as is seen by noticing the different body development that comes with different sports and lifestyles among guys. There certainly are strong cultural components in this. For example, one nowadays sees more guys with bigger triceps (the muscle mass at the back of the upper arm) than before the proliferation of suburban gyms and the lifestyle market that they serve. And the sports clothing market targets accentuated attention to defined male body types

But such recreation and lifestyle choices by guys are also congruent with male psychology. The kinds of physical recreations and fitness and physical performances that guys generally prefer tend to "fit" both their physiology *and* their psychology. In psychological terms, they are "masculine" things that reinforce masculine physiological and psychological instincts, and reinforce "feeling good" about one's masculinity. And the sports clothing – certainly very much a "cultural product" – is generally functional, yet also designed to enhance the geometry of the well-formed masculine body and to motivate guys in "feeling good" about asserting, maintaining, and developing masculine form.

Choices in a culture of feminisation.

There are contrary tendencies to be observed. I suspect that much of the contemporary marketing and advertisement design is not by guys. Gals seem to be confronted by strong male muscularity, and particularly by strong masculine hairiness. And it's now rare to see an advertisement where the male model is not smooth-skinned – very likely by resort to body-shaving or hair-removal creams. This of course can simply be passed-off as "fashion" – and fashion it certainly is. When I was a young man the high-point for the gal viewers in the early "James Bond" *007* movies was where the "star" displayed a big and generously-haired chest. In the contemporary version, the "star" of the "James Bond" re-run is nearer the contemporary models that one sees portrayed in passageway advertisements at airport terminals for designer-label male underwear and designer-label male "fragrances". The early "James Bond" actor would need to apply hair removal cream to the back of his hands to be used in modelling fashion-label watches for men as they appear in such advertising.

These examples instance what I regard as "feminisation" of men by means that contrive to shift the perception of masculinity away from congruence with natural male endowment to a more contrived form. My observations are intended to influence choice in a direction that affirms distinctive masculine physiognomy and physique that enhances natural masculine endowment. That is, to build a congruence between the "natural" and the "cultural" in the masculine identity construct.

Ease with one's masculinity. There is a congruent masculine psychology in this. For example, we expect the haircut of guys to be of a low-maintenance kind, and have a kind of manly unfussiness about it. We expect the choice of clothing by guys to be unfussy, with a clean-cut look that fits a masculine body – and not to be as attention-drawing as the extrovert way that gals often favour. It's part of our sense of manly restraint. This sense of course is inter-psychic or social, but it's also intra-psychic – guys seem less drawn to as overt body display than women. When we wear "shorts", they are not as short as the gear gals seem to prefer. When we have an open-neck look, it's not as revealing as the skimpy tops that gals seem to favour.

One can pick a guy who is at ease with his body, and doesn't try to hide his masculine endowment – and does not adopt the unduly covered-up and buttoned-up look of the guy who lacks masculine ease. All this can happen un-self-consciously. But it can happen – and in some measure perhaps needs to happen – consciously by guys *choosing* an ease with their maleness and choosing to enhance the masculinity of their identity, their presentation of themselves, and their performance. In the matters just briefly surveyed, guys in different life-eras can *choose* identity that marks a manly maturity or a more manly maturity. In so doing they are also affirming, enacting and enhancing their masculine psychology – both in personal or intra-psychic terms and in social or inter-psychic terms. From the "where I come from", this is a choice that is made socially in a male *and* female social world. But firstly it's a choice for *guys* and for the *guy* himself. Guys know themselves and a guy knows himself, and in this aspect a guy needs responsibly to "own" his own identity choice.

Male moderation in social representations. Social representations and episode representations nevertheless influence the ease or unease in such choice. I am often struck, for example, at observing the costume of television presenters. Taking the typical contemporary "interesting" and "personal" interview mode where the female presenter may even be seen in a dress that rides high up her thigh and without stockings and legs crossed, and with a flimsy and low-cut or even super-low-cut top. At such a scene, one could even wonder whether the small clip-on microphone might soon pull down and reveal a nipple, and perhaps even consider whether the colour of her "nickers" would be seen should she uncross her legs! Sitting opposite her and by contrast, the guy is likely to be seen in "male *hijab*" – wearing socks and shoes, a dark suit, white shirt, and a tightly knotted necktie! The contrast with exaggerated Muslim female dress and its implications are intended. Also intended is the highlighting of the different sexual psychology of women that seems to lead them more than men to flaunt their bodies – and to do so more for their own gratification than to please men.

The contrast also highlights the resilience to change in social representation for guys in matters of dress, and the emergence of a seeming normlessness in social representation for gals in matters of dress. This disparity is complex in its intra-psychic and inter-psychic nature. But it underscores that "prescriptiveness" in social representations is not confined to the articulated forms that are found in disciplined organisations such as the Armed Services. "Prescriptiveness" in social representations may occur more widely. The *surprise* that might be expected at this "prescriptiveness" seems to be offset by its "common-place-ness", so that incongruity is not noticed and its tangled psychology usually goes unremarked.

Remarking in the manner just observed serves to highlight that some restraints answer to something inherent in the senses of "fitting", or even of "right" and "wrong". The more prevalent restraints are, however, not of this kind and are better understood in social psychological terms that draw upon inter-psychic understandings of social representations.

What follows from the discourse of this section is that "psychological maturity" does not involve *not* "doing as one pleases", but does involve *moderating* "doing as one pleases". This has been argued in terms of masculine physicality and in the presentation and enactment of masculine physicality in matters such as costume.

The chief psychological generalisation flowing from this discourse is that it is psychological maturity in personal and in social terms that renders such moderation in choice. Psychological maturation involves gaining practice in the poise involved in identifying and enacting suitable flexibility and adaptation within the boundaries of prevailing social representations. Guys face their own distinctive challenges in gaining this poise and in identifying and choosing in these matters an integral *manly maturity*.

Personality and manly maturity

Finding one's own aptitudes for performance and achievement. The previous section focused on "masculinity", rather than on "personality" in terms as earlier treated in the chapter of that title. It is important to reinforce the variety in personalities of guys who nevertheless are "real men", and the ways that different personalities are differently expressed in their manliness. When one travels – and I travel more than most – one cannot but fail to be impressed by the ingenuity and sheer technical excellence of engineers (overwhelmingly male) who as civil engineers were responsible for the design and oversight of amazing roads and bridges; of aeronautical engineers who were responsible for the design and oversight of amazing aircraft; and of maritime engineers for amazing yachts and ships, and so forth. Acquiring this body of knowledge and applying it in ways at once creative and disciplined requires not just the development of intelligence, it also calls upon certain personality traits. They intrigue me, because I am not strong in intelligence of that kind and do not have personality traits that are congruent with that kind of performance and achievement.

I nevertheless do not feel "less male" for lack of the performance and achievement of an accomplished Engineer. My intelligence and aptitudes are more suited to the Social Sciences than to Engineering, and my personality finds more congruence in the domain of "persons" than of "things". As with Engineers, females in the Social Sciences are generally a minority, and often it is congruence between aptitudes and interest – rather than one's sex – that has influenced the discipline choice of women with whom I have worked. My experience in working with women in Social Sciences professional fields has reinforced my view that aptitudes and personality traits are over-lapping sets between guys and gals.

Variety in aptitudes and achievements. The personality and aptitudes congruence for gals generally tends to certain areas of performance and achievement, and for guys generally tends to certain other areas of performance and achievement. But this is a generality – a "tendency" only – and a guy may be a great violinist or a great ballet dancer without this involving his being "un-masculine", while a gal may be a great engineer or an airline pilot without this involving her being "un-feminine". Where we encounter this kind of sexual and gender mobility it does not entail a view that different operational performances are simply "gender neutral". In my professional area I was always conscious – but not "self-conscious" – that my achievements and performances were masculine and that my sex and my gender identification were part of my achievements and performances.

My point is that a guy engaged in occupational activities such as engineering or social sciences and who is at ease with his masculinity should also be at ease in working with gals of like performance and achievement (who nevertheless exercise their performance in ways that are expressive of their sex and gender). This of course presumes that a guy does not have to deal with "sexism" from the gals or with a kind of "feminisation" of the workplace that is dysfunctional to organisational performance. There are, however, other cases that are not so mobile in sex and gender.

Sex-specificity in manliness. Only a man can be a father, and only a woman can be a mother. The growing contemporary failure to accept this "fact of life" is seen in the "gay" / "lesbian" push for civil recognition of same-sex "marriages" and the push for their having children and for nurturing children in same-sex relationships. This push challenges the "given-ness" of human sexuality and the congruence between sex and gender.

A guy does not fulfil paternity merely sexually; he also fulfils his paternity in gender identification and performance. A gal does not fulfil maternity merely sexually; she also fulfils her maternity in gender identification and performance. To confuse these facts is to confuse the integral nature of sex, gender, and person – a confusion that is also detrimental for the responsible nurture of children. There are of course occasions where "Mum" has to supply for "Dad" in his absence, or where "Dad" has to supply for "Mum" in her absence. But these performances are in response to necessity, rather than performances that are to be imputed as normative.

Countering the sex-neutral / gender-neutral push. There, further, are instances where – contrary to the earlier examples involving Engineer or Social Scientist – the sex and gender status restricts performance. It is largely only Catholics and the Orthodox who maintain a male priesthood, and in the face of considerable contemporary cultural challenge – especially for Catholics who are more located in modern Western culture. A "reverse" example using psychological categories rather than theological categories might serve to make the point. Suppose a young man turns up at a monastery of women and declares to the Prioress, "Reverend Mother, I have a burning desire to 'take the veil', and believe that God wants me to be a nun!" The Prioress might well say, "Off with you, you scoundrel!", and that be the end of it. Or she may with more patience say, "Well, you can't be a Sister without being a woman, and you evidently are not that. I think you'd better think through things rather more. Perhaps I can give you some psychological advice?"

The more common contemporary scenario is the woman who wants to be a priest. The Answer is, "Well, you can't be a Father without being a man, and you evidently are not that. I think you'd better think through things rather more. It seems you've not been convinced by the theological reasoning of the doctrine of the Church. Perhaps I can give you a psychological rendering of the 'constant tradition' of the Church?"

My guess is that such psychological "reasoning" also would not "work", because typically in such matters one deals with persons whose adherences are "ideological". To the extent that the reasoning of such persons involves psychology, the dominant perspective is one of simply "cultural construction", and not a perspective that also involves matters that are inherent in human sexuality and inherent to the nature of divine action and disclosure. Some things are difficult to communicate, because some things involve considerable complexity and incongruence with contemporary cultural norms and with personality profiles that are congruent with ascendent contemporary norms.

In a lesser measure, the same problem arises with "male" occupations. Women generally do not wish to become ditch-diggers, sheep-shearers, garbage collectors, or truck drivers. In poor countries one often finds women doing dirty and hard jobs, but they are usually paid much less than men. In countries where "equal pay" applies in one degree or another, men tend to get jobs that are more efficiently done with greater muscularity, with getting very dirty, and with masculine aptitudes in distance/ speed judgements, and so forth.

Tendency to sex and gender concentration in certain aptitudes and performances. My earlier examples were "professional" – Engineers or Social Scientists. I should "balance up" things by saying that I enormously respect those guys whose jobs are hard and dirty – and I enormously respect gals whose jobs are tedious and repetitive. Just imagine what a quandary we would be in if we did not have guys whose aptitudes and accomplishments are of the ditch-digging, and garbage collecting kind! Just imagine what a quandary we would be in if we did not have gals whose aptitudes and accomplishments are of the data-entry or receptionist kind! – not to mention the aptitudes and accomplishments both complex and the mundane of the mothering and home-making kind!

Being mature psychologically does not mean having one set of aptitudes and accomplishments, rather than another. The aptitudes and personality traits differ in kind, in complexity, and in certain respects in level. A guy who is a "professional" is not inherently more mature than a guy who is a "tradesman", and a guy who is a "tradesman" is not inherently more mature than a guy who is a "manual labourer".

Further, we should observe that as cultures and technologies change, so too does the mix of desired aptitudes and achievements. Whoever would have thought when I left school that so many guys with stumpy fingers would need to get these around a computer keyboard, because keyboard skills are so pervasive in contemporary work cultures! I don't even recall that trucks were equipped with power-steering when I was young, and driving a bus required a good deal of masculine muscularity!

Masculine expressiveness in chosen performances. Things have changed. But guys will still do what they do with a masculine expressiveness, and gals will still do what they do with a feminine expressiveness. The maturity issue is whether this "expressiveness" arises from insecurity or whether it is a balanced expression of the way that one's sex and gender integrates with one's personality and thus impacts upon one's aptitudes and achievements. Where that "impact" is healthy and open, one encounters an integrated personality – a "nice guy" or a "gentleman": one encounters a guy whose masculine personality is positively applied in his endeavours, and his various performances display a *manly maturity*.

Psychological development and intellectual development

I do not need in this overview chapter much to amplify what was presented in the chapter titled Developmental Psychology. Suffice to reinforce the point that "development" is a *life-long process*, and that this life-long process involves different things in different life-eras. The notion that one's strengths can be applied to develop one's not-so-strong aptitudes may be manifest even in advanced years – such as where a retired guy takes up activities about which he'd not been confident during his occupational life and enjoys pursuing new aptitudes, even where he does not expect to attain much competence.

Different personalities learn differently and guys learn in masculine ways. It is also worth reinforcing that different personalities learn differently, and thus different personalities have different "developmental" paths. A corollary is that often "catch-up" is possible where earlier learning did not fit the personality. A prime example is where schooling was not "boy friendly" or not "young man friendly" in its curriculum and method – and where "further education" exposures as an emerging adult or as an adult may open-up horizons that were thought of as closed.

Gradation and patience in learning maturation. A sense of gradation and of level is important in opening horizons. Most people move step-wise, and the *pacing* of mental development and of skills development needs to match individual capabilities. And the *level* of mental development and of skills development also needs to match individual capabilities. A guy who, for example, has "missed out" on mathematics education is not necessarily going to become a great mathematician, but he may become a guy who gains a basic maths competence that allows him effectively to manage the basically arithmetic skills as used in everyday life. A guy who never became attuned to literature may become a guy who finds new horizons in literature that open-up his life in surprising ways.

It's also important to reinforce that "intelligence" also is not static. Certainly, guys with more inherent "firepower" have an advantage over those of lesser "firepower". But one cannot over-emphasise the importance of "how a tool is *used*" and "how *tool-like mental skills* are acquired".

Motivation in maturation. Nor can one over-emphasise the importance of *motivation* – the guy with lesser "fire-power" who wants to acquire aptitudes and to demonstrate aptitude performance will often outdo the more gifted guy who is weakly motivated. Building motivation is given impetus where it is presented in masculine terms as the "guy thing to do", as a challenge for guys to build and express identity that is *masculine*.

Social psychology

For most of the discipline history of Psychology the focus has been on the psychology of the person and on intra-psychic processes. Yet most of our psychic functioning is social and involves inter-psychic processes. I suppose that everyone has "off days" and that these may usually be explained by some unidentified physical indisposition. Sometimes, however, the indisposition is unidentified mental indisposition.

To identify an unwellness – whether physical or psychological – is to *name* it. If the psychological unwellness was, say, a matter of *grief*, then naming it as *grieving* makes it not simply intra-psychic but also inter-psychic. Our "namings" are not generally intra-psychic. To "name" is to use language, and to use language is to use social categories. And to arrange social categories in communicable form is to converse. In brief, our thinking is formed by language, and our communication involves language.

Understanding "text" and "reading" text.
The language may be oral or it may be written, textual language or more briefly "text". Our language may also be colour, as in "hot pink" as an erotic colour or "black" as a mourning colour. Our language may be enacted, as in the contemporary phrase "body language" – whether a person is at ease, whether a person struts, whether a person frowns, and so forth. The act of "reading" these different "texts" is *social*. I can read your conversation as "informative", "enquiring", or "explaining". I can read your body language as "calming" or as "arrogant". I can read your accoutrements as "sexy" or "business-like", and so forth. I can read your architecture as "church", "domestic", "utilitarian", and so forth.

All such "readings" are social acts that involve diverse forms of "texts" and diverse forms of "literacy". I intra-psychically may give quite personalised "readings", but communication involves giving social "readings". The performance of social readings and the communication of social readings engages the building of social psychological structures and the building of competencies in the employment of psychological structures. In brief, it involves inter-psychic processes.

Building inter-psychic structures. Maturity in social psychology thus involves the over-time building of inter-psychic structures in the person and in the social group and the gaining of competency in their use. To speak simply in a linguistic metaphor, maturity in social psychology involves learning a language and gaining fluency in the language learned. Continuing further in linguistic terms, some people have strong language aptitudes and given opportunity may become multi-lingual. Others may have lesser language aptitudes and remain mono-lingual and have simpler language structures and smaller word vocabularies. The latter tend to socialise in a single group and to use only the language of a single group and to be confined to the thought patterns of a single group. The former may socialise more widely – across classes from high-brow to low-brow, from technical and abstract to concrete and more every-day, from national to inter-national, and so forth.

Maturity not "high-brow" / "low-brow". Whether in such a perspective one is or is not "mature" depends mainly upon the degree of sensience. One might not be conversant with a wider world or with a more sophisticated world, but if one is able to say, "Well, I'm not very informed on what 'they' do, but from 'where I come from' this seems to me to be silly." Such a remark portrays a person who within his framework has thought-through his position, and who yet recognises the provisional nature of his position, and who makes his judgements and communicates his judgements with some appreciation of their limitations.

This may be contrasted with the person of wide cross-cultural experience and more sophisticated world-views, but who says, "Well, I know what I am talking about and this rabble does not and simply does not deal with the complexity and the technicality of the issue." Such a remark portrays a person who uses high-sounding language but without careful thought and without relating it to the experience of people whose worldviews and experiences are unsophisticated. It is the latter who in psychological terms may be socially *immature* and the former who in psychological terms may be socially *mature*.

Courage, openess, and generosity in building maturity. As with intelligence, those with more "firepower" have advantage – but advantage does not determine the outcome. So also, those with greater language diversity, fluency, and complexity have advantage – but advantage does not determine the outcome. Building a social psychology that is *mature*, and, in masculine terms, that has *manly maturity* is precisely a "building" activity. It is an activity that takes time; takes persistence; takes taking opportunities for experience; takes courage; takes an open-ness and a generosity. Much of this illustrative list involves matters of "character", and character is formed over time and by habitual choices – mostly virtuous choices – and thus the psychology of building social psychological maturity is complex and multi-faceted.

Emotional maturity

Priority of "affect" in cultural reading. In speaking of social psychology I resorted to the "text" language of Cultural Studies as developed in academic literary contexts (such as English as an academic discipline) where "text" is given a generic meaning – such as "reading" the text of a particular architectural structure like a war memorial or an office block. Much of such textual reading calls not firstly upon cognitive faculties, but firstly upon faculties that in psychological terms are termed affective or *affect*.

Whatever a person is articulating, whether it is said with a frown or with a smile or with neutral expression is usually noticed and processed *before* more cognitive processing is completed. In noticing a particular architectural structure, the emotional response of "like" or "dislike" is likely to proceed before the more congitive response of "utilitarian" or "inconvenient", and so forth.

I noted that study of the psychology of the person underwent more discipline development before discipline development of the social psychology. It further is so that social psychology as a cognitive discipline underwent more discipline development before the social psychology of affect. In each case, the late-comer is the more important discipline in practical terms.

Affect and inter-psychic processes. This is so because inter-psychic processes seem generally more determinative than intra-psychic processes, and affective processes seem generally more determinative psychologically than cognitive processes. Most people more quickly respond to affect than to cognition. Usually, people will decide whether they like or dislike a person before they decide whether they agree or disagree with what the person is saying. Affect generally impacts more directly than does cognition. This is an important psychological recognition.

It follows that the psychologically astute person – whether consciously or unconsciously – will first "read" the affective disposition of the person or persons with whom communication is engaged. This emotional "reading" will strongly influence – or even dictate – what is *said* and what is *not said*; and *how much* is said and *how much is not said*;

and *how* what is said is said; and *when* to say what one is to say; and the *voice tonality* of what is said; and whether it is said in *oral* terms or in *literary* terms (text "text"), and so forth. All such issues can be thought about in a *cognitive* manner, but they are likely first to be thought about in an *affective* manner.

Building affective competencies. It takes time and experience to build these affective competencies. Some have more advantage than others – that is what is implied in my treating the preference for "feeling" or "thinking" processes in the opening chapter on Personality. But those who have less-advantage in a "firepower" sense are nevertheless able to "work at" these aptitudes and competencies. Because affect figures so prominently in communication, developing affective aptitudes and competencies becomes crucial for developing psychological maturity.

Gendering affective competencies. These affective attributes will be both sexed and gendered. That is, the gendering of the behaviour needs a congruence with the sex of the acting person. When we hear expressions such as *butch* of a gal, it may just mean "She's a bit of a 'tomboy'" or "She has a rather short and severe haircut". More generally, it usually means an unpleasing affective perception of a lack of femininity. When we hear the term *effeminate* of a guy, it may just mean "He wears his hair in a flouncy way" or "He giggles like a girl". More generally, it usually means an unpleasing affective perception of a lack of masculinity. In brief, affective maturity for a guy involves *manly affective maturity*.

This means that guys in developing affective aptitudes

and competencies need to attend to the language of gender. Gals tend to get "front desk" jobs not simply because on-job skills induction can be brief and job-tenure shorter, but because gals are more disposed to smile than guys, and this "works better" in initial customer relations. Likewise in telephony work, gals tend to have higher recognition of voice tonality than guys, and thus better to smooth customer relations. Gals tend more to choose Social Work than guys, and affective cognitions figure prominently in that profession. Many similar examples could be instanced.

Guys expect from a guy different affective responses than from a gal. Just think about how you'd handle the introductory meeting in a house visit by a tradesman as compared with a "cleaning lady" – and you'll quickly see that there are subtle gender issues in the different social communications. It is often the gals who will have more aptitude in matters of the psychology of affect – ask any male manager who has a good working relationship with a female personal secretary, and you are likely to hear testimony of astute advice given!

Male-female collaboration in building affective competencies. A corollary of the above examples is that building affective aptitudes and performances for guys often benefits from male-female collaboration, or female-male collaboration. But this building of affective aptitudes and performances in guys has also to attend to their masculine expression. The congruence between sex and gender matters a lot in the affective realm.

A word of caution, however, is that a sense of even-handedness has to be preserved – gals will hate a condescending attitude from guys, and so will guys from gals. Personal courtesy is always important. What is "courteous" will vary immensely and require astute affective judgements – "Give me a break, honey!" (said to a gal) and "Get off my back, you bastard!" (said to a guy) are colloquial and gendered examples that may seem "rude", but in gender relations contexts may be quite courteous words of moderation or, alternatively, insultingly intemperate when context-inappropriate. Discerning one from the other is a matter of *emotional maturity*. And this emotional maturity often involves differing discernments by sex and gender.

Moral psychology

Postmodernist focus on context. In the chapter on maturity in moral psychology emphasis was placed on the *content* and *context* aspects of moral cognition and decision. In a postmodernist society, there is a marked need to reinforce *content* in moral cognition and decision. Yet sound moral cognition and decisions need both deductive and inductive method – they at once should be syllogistically tight *and* empirically grounded (or at least as syllogistically tight as fits the diversity of the issue and at least as empirically grounded as the issue is tractable to such approaches).

At times it can be exceedingly difficult to adjudge the empirical circumstances. Capital punishment (the "death penalty") is an example where there is something approaching a general consensus in Western societies against its use. It is not a consensus with which I agree, but the more pertinent issue is "context" where across most of the world it is not possible in practical terms to maintain incarceration conditions that are humane and secure. Poor countries simply cannot afford humane gaols when a significant proportion of their populations live in humanly degraded conditions. Countries where civil order is weakly established simply cannot reliably provide secure incarceration. This is an instance where the *practical* considerations – apart from the more abstract moral reasonings – mean that more "grounded" moral reasonings decisions are required.

On the other hand, instrinsic moral reasonings are often weak. Great lengths are gone to in juridical and penitentiary processes for *post-partum* killing of children, and yet *ante-natal* killing of children (abortion, pregnancy termination) is generally quarantined from juridical and penitentiary processes. The push *not to know* the facts about abortion is seen in the decrying of graphic depiction of aborted foetuses (pictures showing their physiological development), or data analyses showing the demographic implications of widespread pregnancy terminations.

This is a pressing example of widespread denial of empirical facts surrounding a moral issue – a widespread desire for empirical ignorance. This arises from a widespread refusal to reckon with the intrinsic nature of the action – the termination of a viable *in utero* human life. Both context *and* content of the moral decision are denied. As individuals, most persons "do not want to know" and as a society, most people "do not want to know". And, generally speaking, there is a social consensus on this intended "not knowing". Mainly, it is simply that the truth is "inconvenient" and the implications of the truth are "inconvenient".

Inconvenience of intrinsic morality. This is the problem with an intrinsic morality – it is not very amenable to "consensus", because its claims are of an "in and of itself" kind. Morality that is "objective" challenges us to moral observance that we might not like and that society may not like. This is the primary contemporary conflict in moral psychology.

What people "do not want to know" they generally do not think through – either cognitively or affectively. It thus requires a resilience and courage on the part of someone who *does* undertake the thinking through of moral issues that persons, organisations, or society prefer to ignore.

This kind of thinking through and the consequent advocacy and argumentation are not likely to win popularity. "Virtue" will mainly be prized when it affirms persons, organisations, or society – that is, where it reflects the prevailing social representations of uprightness.

True virtue may bring disapprobation, rather than approbation, and the processes of psychological exclusion that follow. The virtuous may be harassed, may be ridiculed, and may be socially and psychologically marginalised.

Moral robustness is built psychologically. This calls for great robustness and subtlety on the part of those whose who seek "moral" behaviour, rather than simply "ethical" behaviour. A stable robustness does not just "happen" – it is cultivated psychologically, both intra-psychically and inter-psychically. And pursuing a moral program requires perseverance and subtlety.

This subtlety involves the careful and balanced reasoning of the relevant moral structure and their contextual circumstances; the shrewd adjudging of what supporting arguments are most likely to gain traction; and the shrewd judgement of what affective appeals are most likely to persuade. Without this subtlety, the moral person may well be ostracised for what others see as "being objectional", rather than "being reasonable". These complex aptitudes and performances do not just "happen". They are the result of maturation processes, including psychological maturation. And growth and maturation of these complex aptitudes and performances only arise where motivation is sustained, including motivation in intra-psychic and in inter-psychic terms.

For most people this maturation will draw upon support networks that are personal (such as deep friendships) and organisational (such as moral project associations). This raises its own difficulties. Friends may depart when the "going gets tough or too tough"; moral project organisations may find other agendas more pressing and dump those who are dysfunctional to the "other agendas". This last observation applies particularly in church organisations – members may prefer their social cosiness or their reputational probity, rather than costly performance of moral choice. More focused organisations may move in ideological directions that simplistically and self-righteously uphold a certain moral agenda.

Psychological hazards in not "going with the flow". These are the various dynamics that can sap vigour in pursuing a moral program, and lead to psychological distress and isolation. Adjudging the psychological "maturity" or the "*im*maturity" of those who pursue moral programs needs to make recognition of the psychological hazards of "swimming against the stream". These are refined judgements, and those who adjudge the performances of those seeking virtue need to be alert that the pathway in virtue is hazardous and requires practice and learnings – not least psychological learning.

Masculine toughness in pursuing issues complex conceptually and psychologically.

I so far have perhaps not spoken sufficiently widely in sex and gender terms. Evidently, when something is complex conceptually and psychologically, it calls upon a variety of psychological aptitudes and performances – and these are usually best developed and delivered in collaboration between men and women. But men tend more to emphasise cognitive issues in their justice deliberations, while women tend more to emphasise relational issues in their justice deliberations. The manly contribution often is strongly to push through the cognitive issues in their rigour and complexity.

I do not under-estimate the toughness that women can display in pursuing a moral program. But neither do I under-estimate the importance of masculine toughness in pursuing a moral program. There are more ways to be a warrior than carrying a sword or a gun, and the guy who pursues a moral program will need warrior skills and will need to develop warrior character – and as a mature man he is likely to be a "battle scarred warrior"! There is a masculine quality in the pursuit of personal virtue and social virtue – there is a *manly maturity in moral psychology*.

Role of self-restraint and moderation in pursuing personal maturity.

The two chapters on immaturity among men that preceded the present chapter are nearer for reader recall, and do not so much need re-statement. The obvious points are the *un*manliness in the virtue sense of the autocrat and the coward, and the *un*manliness of the covert practice of social exclusion and of moral disengagement and moral self-deception. I shall reinforce manliness in sexual conduct and expression in the late chapter dealing with Psychological Dynamics. Suffice here simply to re-state that the development of manly maturity requires the development of self-restraint, moderation, and right direction of masculine sexual instincts and drives. Social psychological processes may act by way of inhibiting dysfunctional acting-out of those instincts, but do not fully supply where virtuous development of masculine dignity and responsibility in matters sexual has not been engaged. This virtuous development in guys should be understood in psychological terms as the development of *manly maturity*.

Summing-up: maturity as work-in-progress

A chapter under a title of Overview Perspectives of necessity involves some "broad brushing" across a wide range. The very range covered – cultural considerations; personality; intellect; social aptitudes and skills; affective psychology; moral psychology – implies that the psychological processes of this development *take time*. Psychological maturity across a wide front does not occur either quickly or evenly.

In some respects maturity can be a "state" condition (something achieved), but maturity more often is a "process" condition (a work-in-progress). And as a work-in-progress, certain components will be more progressed than others; and certain components will need to be re-learned; and certain components will need up-dating for congruence with different age-life-eras and with changes in cultural content and cultural context.

While maturity brings costs (even heavy costs), implicitly I underscore that maturity mostly brings pleasure (like the pleasure of mature wine). The costliness of maturity is so because dealing with immaturity in others becomes more tiresome, and, indeed, more burdensome as greater demands are made upon one's psychological resources. And not infrequently, maturity also brings the burden of the discomfort suffered where it attracts immature reaction and even the psychology of exclusion. Nevertheless, manly maturity is suffused with joy, and *joy* is the last sentence of the end notes for the concluding chapter of this book.

Perhaps the most abiding satisfaction of the maturing experience is the way it equips one to help others – to mentor others. I have spent the greater part of my life as a teacher, and I have enjoyed the classroom and enjoyed my own academic achievements and those of my students. But the greatest joy has been what has not been "teaching", but has been "mentoring" – the non-formal or informal being available as a mature man to boys and emerging young men as they have grappled with their own aspirations, inhibitions, set-backs, and struggles to claim their own *manly maturity*. The next chapter is directed to outlining some pointers on how to be a *man for others*, especially a man for those who engage *emerging manhood*. Disappointments and failures will be encountered in this mentoring, but it is the pleasure at seeing a fine boy (or even a not-so-fine boy) become a fine emerging adult, and a fine emerging adult become a fine young man that is an enduring gift and fruit of one's own work-in-progress for *manly maturity*.

11
Manly Mentoring for Maturity

Introduction

The most important mentoring influence is the whole-life one: simply the presence among boys and young men of older guys who implicitly reinforce a sense of virile manliness. Yet direct activity and conversational mentoring remains important, especially for boys and young men. This section offers some advice under 15 headings on enacting this direct conversational and activity mentoring, starting off with the most important precept.

Keeping "your agenda" out of it. First remember that any mentoring is to help the one whom you are mentoring (the mentoree). This means that something that is "for you" (*your* "agenda") has largely to be out-of-the picture.

A crucial thing also to be out-of-the-picture is any lewd sexual interest by yourself in the younger person being mentored. If this is not the case, then *"Don't"*. An older person cannot help a younger person in circumstances where the younger person is an object of sexual interest. In using the term "object of sexual interest", I, of course, mean of lewd sexual interest. I do not mean that one does not admire the younger person as a fine specimen of emerging manhood, where that admiration is part of one's sense of the nobility of the younger person.

Respect his freedom. The second thing to remember is to avoid a situation where the younger person feels "cornered". After all, if you are offering help to a younger person, then he should be able to opt-out, to decide, "No thanks." That means you need to choose circumstances where the younger person can walk out or walk away. And you need to take a conversational tack where you receive signals from the younger person that it's okay to keep moving forward in the direction to which you've alluded, and to "back off" where you don't receive those signals.

Be prudent for yourself. The third thing to remember is to maintain a prudent sense of your own protection. I do not mean protection from someone who may be physically stronger than yourself. I mean protection from detraction. You must assess whether there is a basic trust relationship between you and the young person. In charting your course, you need to consider whether what you say and the way you say might be misrepresented by the young person you are helping. This is hazardous, because people young and old who do not have emotional maturity and moral maturity can wreak havoc in misrepresenting some engagement in negative tones – even to the point of presenting something positive and restrained as "reportable conduct" under state Child Protection legislation. This difficulty is not addressed by establishing "secrecy", because secrecy is a prime tack among those who have perverse purposes and who may be grooming a young person for later sexual advances. It is, rather, making prudent judgement that what you say would be judged on calm reasoning as appropriate to the circumstances and age-appropriate to the young person involved.

Choosing the venue and occasion. The fourth thing is the actual setting of the engagement. Publicity about cases of sexual interference by older persons of younger persons has generated a heightened suspicion and suspiciousness nowadays, and this may make it harder to find appropriate settings.

A bush camp for boys now becomes charged if the older person is, say, sharing a tent or dormitory-style sleeping accommodation. Where the venue is a sleeping area (whether at a camp or in a house), prudence would generally dictate the presence of another and responsible older man, and not being in a situation where it is just you alone and the younger person, rather than two or more younger persons. This is a constraint, because talking across beds when lights are out can often be a helpful setting for communicating on sensitive topics. But nowadays one is more constrained, and one needs to take care that situations that are more open to depiction in ways that reflect on your integrity are adjudged soberly.

It is better that settings be clear of sleeping areas. It is better that settings be open, rather than closed. Often one needs privacy to pursue a delicate conversation, but the privacy is better of a kind where there is a physical remove such that someone approaching can see that this is a conversation not to be disturbed or where you can simply say, "We'll join you soon, Jack; Jim and I just need to close this conversation." A verandah setting is a good example, because it is open to others' inspection, but others can't approach all of a sudden. It is better for you to be able to say, "That conversation can't be construed as 'grooming'; I was talking only about what an older person such as myself might reasonably speak with a younger person." Where the young person is an adult, the prudential considerations are not as great. But most young men at 18 are still going to be somewhat boy-like, and one should not assume adult stability. There's a big difference between the ways that one might relate with a young man in early-twenties whose self-identity is stable as compared with the ways one might relate with a young man who by age and personality may be more vulnerable in matters of personal identity, including sexual identity. One needs the maturity soberly to adjudge such differences.

Age-appropriate issues. The fifth thing to ask is whether the speaking is age-appropriate? A very real problem for the maturation process is speaking occurring too late. This is particularly so with primary-school age children. I doubt that in any era that children waited until puberty for stirring of their sexual interest. This certainly is not so now. Boys will often quite cheekily reveal what they want to know about, and nowadays it can be a fine judgement as to what is age-appropriate. It follows from your not yourself having a sexual interest in the young person that you can better assess what the young person knows already, what the young person is curious about, and just how much communication is going to best fit the young person or young persons in the situations encountered.

Manner of speaking. The sixth thing is your own manner of speaking. I think it's best not to give what seems like a lesson in physiology. Perhaps you might use the term "penis", but it will generally be more appropriate to use the term that the young person would use. That doesn't mean, for example, that you loosely use the term "cunt", because it usually has derogatory associations. But terms such as "dick", "backside", "stiff" or "hard-on", for example, will generally allow boys or young men to talk about sexual matters in a way that is matter-of-fact and comfortable, and realistic, rather than clinical. It's important by your language to convey a sense that sex, while a delicate matter, is not something to evoke shame. Your manner of speaking needs to convey a sense that sex is an everyday matter that everyone has to deal with in a way that retains both dignity and straight-forwardness.

Moral issues in speaking. The seventh thing is to speak in a way that conveys a sense that sex is a moral issue. I don't imply that it's "sex", "sex", "sex" about which we should converse. It is, rather, that sex is a central topic for the emerging adult, and it's a necessary but delicate topic and a moral topic. It's *not* a moral issue that a boy's testicles drop; that he gets erections; that he emits semen; that he has erotic dreams and sleeping ejaculations; that he's interested in others' sexuality, and especially in girls' sexuality.

What is moral is how he *governs* his sexual instincts. And by "governs", I do not mean *represses*. I mean how he acts out his sexual instincts and sexual urges. That means that an older person needs to convey to a boy or young man (or boys-to-boys and young-men-to-young-men in peer-to-peer situations) that sex essentially is like all our faculties. Our sexual faculties can be *used* or *abused*. It's important not to have notions of "abuse" that are too crude; it's important to convey a sense that making judgements in matters sexual often requires some discernment. But that discernment is not simply conventional ("what every one else is doing"), but something that must be worked through – with discernment that involves the kind of moral reasoning involved in ethical and moral education. And, as I see it, also worked through with prayer of the kind that lays all before God and seeks understanding and grace – not grace that supplants nature, but where "grace builds upon nature", including sexual nature.

Strengthening virtuous choice. The eighth thing to remember is that when you are engaging a young person on matters sexual, you are trying to strengthen the capacity of the young person to appreciate both the matter-of-factness of his sexuality and the dignity of his sexuality. You thus need to be at once down-to-earth and somewhat elevated. And you need to give the young person a sense of making choices, and making choices responsibly, and making choices that are both realistic and moral. I've had more to say about moral choices in the chapter on Moral Psychology. But one needs to be alert that this is not just a matter of "psychology", but a matter of what is good and what is not good. Life's choices have to be about *virtue*, and engaging a young person on matters sexual needs to propose to a young person the ways to strengthen capacity to discern what is virtuous and to enact what is virtuous.

Priority of personal responsibility. The ninth thing is to remember throughout is that this manner of engaging a young person needs so far as possible to sustain a conversational tone. That is, you need to minimise teaching in a didactic sense, and attempt to teach by engaging the young person in conversation. This means being alert to the opportunities for the young person to articulate his understanding, and for you to take up the language that he uses in order to reinforce what you think needs reinforcing.

I have said "he" because I am here speaking about boys and young men, but I could say "they", because there will be contexts where such conversations are best had with a group (preferably, generally with a same-sex group). Where the conversation is with a group, then the group can act to reinforce shared appreciation of conversation on sexual matters. Where this is appropriate, one may thereby be able to cultivate group reinforcement of virtuous behaviour. But one needs to take care that one does not reinforce group conformity, because the priority of personal responsibility and morality that involves personal identification and adherence is so important. After all, each young person is being helped to take charge of his own life.

Avoid condescension. The tenth thing takes up the last point made. We are speaking about the nobility of the young person. This means that there is no place for condescension. One does not win trust by putting-down. And one does not win trust by putting a "cliff" in front of a young person. All that is said should be thought of in "pathway" terms. A mentor needs to extend and challenge, but always in a manner that is kindly, rather than daunting.

Such extending and challenging needs to reflect your personal consistency in understanding and in life enactments. The young guy needs your stability, including stability in the face of adversity. This means recognising where the young person is now, and proposing a pathway ahead that is graduated and that will stimulate – rather than exhaust – the one who undertakes and perseveres on that pathway.

The respect for the young person also respects what is possible, and acknowledges graduation in moving forward, and reinforces a strengthening so that moving forward can be sustained. One of the best things that a young guy ever said to me is, "Father, you don't say *Do this*, but *Let's do this*." That is, he affirmed a sense of my companioning him. Young guys growing to maturity need to encounter older guys as "getting alongside them", rather than standing above them. This kind of respect for the young guy build-ups his identity while not over-aweing him. It's got to be realistic and at ease – including at ease on matters sexual. My adage is, "Be relaxed, but not lax."

Doing physical things together. The eleventh thing I would mention is physical engagement – doing things together that have a manly robustness. Activities such as running, hiking, boating, gym work, and team sports such as touch football and sports coaching that place physical demands upon you and where the young person may outclass you, but still respect you as a vigorous man, build confidence among younger persons that you are a man to be emulated. You cannot simply be a buddy in the peer-to-peer sense, but you can be a buddy in a man-to-man sense, and physical engagement helps keep healthy an overall manly mentoring. And the meal and the drinks together round-out the enjoyment of and reflection upon a wide sense of manliness, and strengthen the social aspects of the maturation process.

Cultural exposure. The twelfth thing I would mention, like the eleventh, is not really "well down the list". Maturing young people need sound cultural stimulation and education. Culture of course covers a wide field, but I here speak of the kind of cultural experience that many miss out on. How many boys and young men read during their youthful years a book like Homer's *The Odyssey?* It's a book set in a world far apart from ours, but a book that sets before the boy or young man reader the journey and the vista of searching for his father and of finding his own manhood.

A big part of the problem of guys not reading arises because as boys and young men they were not exposed to literature that can stir their manliness, and help them to advance their own engagement with becoming a mature man. And this is true across the whole field of higher culture. A symphony concert overture like *1812* has the kind of emotional texture that can enter the soul of a young man and stir his sense of valour. Paintings like those of Caravaggio stirringly depict the turmoil and the struggle in enacting manhood. A Ballet like Khatachurian's *Sparticus* gives the male form a heroic depiction that stirs a young man to "walk tall" and to appreciate manly vigour. And all such things are infused with moral purpose that strengthen both the aspiration for and the momentum to move forward in manly purpose and dignity.

This can also involve creating occasions where a young guy can dress more formally. How often do you see a young guy on occasions such as a wedding or a funeral when part of his discomfort is just that he's not used to seeing himself in dress clothing, not used to a culture of dress other than knock-about gear. A mentor needs to nurture a wider sense of the cultural horizons of manliness.

Widening horizons and stepping out. The last two points have emphasised a sense of vista. An approach that is like a closed-in counselling session is by itself not going to provide the opening-up momentum to see and appreciate the wide vista that is involved in manly maturation. Maturation also involves "stepping out of oneself", a looking out and up. It's an adventure, and needs to be approached adventurously. Manly mentoring needs to be adventurous, and to involve adventurous activities – whether ones that enhance the physical stamina, intellectual stamina, social stamina, or cultural adventurousness. A successful mentor is ready to propose adventure to his mentoree and to take up the challenge presented by a young guy and allowing him and/or his peers to take leadership with the benefit of the presence and mature experience of an older guy or older guys.

Guys and gals socialisation. I've necessarily given such a male emphasis in presenting mentoring of boys and young men. This is all going to be lop-sided unless it is infused with a reverent attitude toward girls and young women, and a lively sense of guys and gals socialisation. As I've said from the start, one can't respect boys and young men without respecting girls and young women. Mentoring needs also an aspect of gaining social ease with both guys and gals.

Manly mentoring is one where the older guy implicitly and at times explicitly conveys a lively sense of "male and female, in his own image God created man", and where this is manifest in every-day and practical ways. Guys who mature in manly dignity have a deep respect for gals and for womanly dignity, and for the beauty of humanity that is male and female. Without this sense, guy-to-guy mentoring will lack a genuinely manly robustness.

The implicit foundations of your own manliness. I've made a lot of points, but the last one is to touch upon a sense both of honour and of humility. Boys and young men need to encounter a man of honour if he is to be a mentor. They don't need to encounter a man who is "perfect", and who is unwilling to expose in appropriate ways his own learning from mistakes and his own vulnerabilities. They do need to encounter a man who has a keen sense of grace from God. The simply self-achieving man ends up being an arrogant man. The man who understands and practices the precept "grace builds upon nature" can be a humble man. And a humble man has a dignity that is truly manly and that attracts emulation.

"Last Words". In writing or speaking in this vein, one comes up with "last words", and the "last words" can multiply. Often we learn from those whom we've helped, and incisive words spoken to me by an emerging adult have really stayed with me: "I am really grateful, Father, that you gave me space and time; space and time to grow. I'm really grateful for that." So don't try to hasten things. Work with a near-horizon objective and with a longer-horizon objective, and give the young guy space and time to fill his own horizon. As I said at the beginning of this enumeration, the "agenda", after all, is not yours, but *his*.

Strategy in Mentoring

As just emphasised, it is crucial for the mentor to maintain a sense that "It's the young guy's life", and to support an agenda that is *his*. It nevertheless remains crucial for the mentor to have a sense of direction that is instrumental – to develop and over time to convey a sense of *strategy*.

A life lived without strategy will have little direction, and mentoring undertaken without strategy will lack progression. The "mentoring tips" so far treated in this chapter arise from my own experience. The term "emerging adult" that I have often adopted is drawn from the work on the psychology of maturation developed under the title *Emerging Adults* by Jeffrey Arnett. The next five sub-sections draw on Arnett's thoughtful "scaffolding" of the transition to adulthood. The five scaffolding pillars that he proposes for strategic interventions are: planful competence; future orientation; motivation to change; successful mentoring; and positive engagement in age-salient tasks. I make a few remarks of my own on each of these features.

Planful competence. Often a plan has to be bold to bring about change. But mostly transitions need to be progressive, and the progress needs to be *planned*. Strategic mentoring for transition to adulthood needs to engage the younger guy in the planning exercise. The younger guy needs by example and conversation and action to be able to imagine, to be able to talk through and think through, and to be able to enact a progressive plan that brings about a transition to maturity – and a kind and image or vision of maturity to which he aspires. The older guy's task is to companion the younger guy in building the competencies involved in a planful approach toward "where he is going" ("where we are going").

Future orientation. Such a planful competence must have a future orientation. A mentor is going to be most strategically significant where the younger guy is coming from circumstances where his own imaginings have not been cultivated or where they have been thwarted. Such a past is not to be denied, nor even necessarily decried, but there has to be a perspective of "we're moving on" ("*you're* moving on"). The future is not conformed to the past. It's the future that most holds the promise, and the promise of the future is a promise that in important respects one can enact.

In important respects one can be master of one's own future; one can make a desired future happen; one can by thoughtful scaffolding and through understanding constructional processes create one's future: one can "dream", and one can *fulfil one's dream*. This is the confidence that a mentor has to cultivate in working with emerging adults.

Motivation to change. There are many resources that one needs to achieve a successful transition to mature manhood. But none is more crucial than the inward resource of one's own motivation. The mentor has to cultivate self-confidence in the younger guy; has to encourage the early signs of positive self-identity and recognition of emerging self-confidence; has to portray the kinds of futures that can be chosen and the pathways toward implementation of choices.

Where a mentor discerns a wholesome desire, there needs to be a reinforcement of: "examine this"; "explore this"; "identify the first steps"; "position yourself for the first steps"; and *"go for it!"* Motivation to change is cultivated by inspiring; by encouraging imagination; by cheering the early achievements; by *believing* that the young guy can be instrumental in his moving forward.

Successful mentoring. Whenever one chooses an enumeration, there will be overlap, and the role of "successful mentoring" in the thoughtful scaffolding of the transition processes to manly maturity has already been somewhat canvassed. The essential point to reinforce is that a guy who has in some measure "made it" needs to have a heart for the young guy who is still making the transition, and a readiness for pro-actively engaging with the younger guy in the transition process.

It is a huge privilege to share one's experience and what one has learned (one's wisdom) as one companions a younger guy on the path to mature manhood. The term "mentoring" has already been given some content in this chapter. Perhaps "companioning" is a key to understanding successful mentoring, because *companioning* carries a sense of walking with, rather than directing or walking ahead. The descriptor "successful" implies that the mentoring acts *instrumentally* in the transition process so that the younger guy is able to enact and to own his own achievements.

Positive engagement in age-salient tasks. The phrase "thoughtful scaffolding of strategic interventions for understanding the transition processes" is adapted from Arnett. The language is instructive, because it combines both reflection or thought *and* action. Thought and action need to be address to "Where the young person is at" in order to be instrumental for change.

The very phrase "transition" implies not a discrete step, but *process*, and only where each step is salient or relevant both to "where one is coming from" and "where one is going" will it be instrumental for the transition to mature manhood.

One can think of "age-salient" for a young teenager and "age-salient" for a late-teenager. But really, the understanding of "age-salient" needs to be more comprehensive. Some young teenagers in some respects may already have late-teenager competencies, while some late-teenagers may in certain areas have only early-teenager competencies. The "competencies" may be physical development, social development, cognitive development, for example. It's really a case of accurate identification of what are the developmental tasks and when to stage the development tasks.

Evidently also, identified developmental tasks need to be located in cultivating of "planful competence"; need to be located in a forward-looking or "future orientation" perspective; need to be integrated with and supported by "motivation for change"; need to be supported by "successful mentoring"; and thereby to provide a scaffolding that supports the successful transition to mature adulthood. Evidently, these generalisations apply as much to gals as to guys, but the context for the present consideration is *manly maturity* – and so in manner of thinking and enactment, applications need to relate to and to appeal to masculine psychology.

Manly love

Some years back, I remember my surprise when an older man spoke to me disparaging the hugging and ruffling of hair between team mates on the football field or the cricket pitch as they celebrated achievements in the game. He expected that there should be only a sober handshake between men. I didn't know what to say, because what he decried seemed to me to be a healthy expression of guys together enjoying one another. Their tactile expressions of pleasure and joy seemed to me to be of a *Love ya man!* kind, and not something effeminate or kinky. I didn't know what to say, because I respected this older gentleman's way, but it seemed to me to be stilted.

Certainly, nowadays any older guy who gets involved with younger guys may get looked at askance – and looked at askance not just from a dated stiltedness, but with suspicion. The suspicion may be a "political correctness" that does not allow relaxed relationship between older and younger guys, or suspiciousness that implies degraded motives in such relationships. People who so look askance and who talk askance usually have little or no appreciation of *manly love*.

Yet it is manly love that is being enacted in the mentoring relationship that is described in this chapter. The word "love" takes many meanings in English usage, and it is important not to eclipse its most noble usage. This is where one's thought and action is directed first to the welfare of another and first to respect for and honouring of another – especially in ways that are instrumental for ennobling the other. This mentoring love of course is not a "men only" love, and older women of course also mentor younger women in a womanly manner with womanly love.

But the thought and action of guys has its own masculine quality, and what is being proposed in this chapter is the love expressed by older guys for younger guys when they think and act as manly mentors. This kind of love is not possessing. The relationship may take qualities of friendship, even of enduring friendship. A mentoring relationship becomes unhelpful if erotic interest or attachment enters, and it is the responsibility of the mentor to see that this does not grow and quietly to restrain any such stirrings on the part of the mentoree. This is especially so as mentoring often involves guiding in matters sexual, and certainly in matters of sexual identity, and in this – as in other areas – the disinterested moral leadership of the mentor is crucial.

As the younger guy becomes more self-confident in his self-identity, the relationship may fade. Gratitude for the mentoring may remain, but the love offered by a mentor is directed toward younger guys finding their own identity and their own way in life. A wholesome mentoring always respects this governing principle.

Those who would degrade or look askance or talk askance at the healthy and natural manners of relating involved in mentoring for manly maturity in fact inhibit and decry manly *love*. The love depicted in this chapter is far removed from smoochiness and from self-indulgence and certainly from depravity. Love thinks and acts with a disinterested generosity and seeks the welfare and the nobility of the other. "Manly mentoring for maturity" enacts such love.

Those whose manly maturity has been helped by this manly love will find much reward in extending their good fortune to younger generations. Those whose manly maturity has been more struggled will find much reward in making easier the pathways to manly maturity for younger guys. Love does not eagerly look for rewards, but nevertheless does bring its own rewards. Boyhood (like girlhood) is a wonderful era in a person's life. But it is not an enduring era. Seeing a boy achieve the transition from boyhood to manhood (including in its travail) is a joy that is the reward of the love that is *manly mentoring*.

12

Manliness and Womanliness in Maturity

Introduction: understanding "equality"

It is a "hard call" in our present cultural situation to speak under the topic of manliness and womanliness. This was less so when I was growing up. In that era, "Man" meant the race ("God made man, in the image of God, male and female he created them"), and man also meant a male of the race. When it meant the race, it was often capitalised (*Man*) and when it meant one man it was not capitalised (*man* for singular and *men* for plural). But *men* could also be used in the generic ("For us men and our salvation", as in the Creed). Similarly, the personal pronoun *he* could be used both singularly or generically ("He said such and such" referring to a boy or a man, "He should pay attention to the text", meaning either a male or a female reader). The use of "their" and "they" for a singular subject would have been marked "incorrect", while nowadays one often encounters a politically correct "he or she", or a grammatically incorrect "they".

The lead in this linguistic change has been a "feminist" push that decries an earlier understanding of the identity of men in the race Man, with this earlier understanding and behaviour decried as "sexist". This conflict is a tangled one, and has elements that are helpful, and elements that are unhelpful.

I think it's generally a good thing that there should be a basic identity in the civic rights of males and females of our race. Among those who do not describe themselves as "feminists", few would question the right of female citizens to the vote, to hold a drivers' licence, to study and practice medicine or engineering, and so forth. But it is only the ideologically driven who do not identify certain boundaries to sexual equality.

"Equality" is not always "mathematical": men and women are "equal", but they are not always the same in their equality. Those who not recognise this to be the case think, for example, that the Australian Army discriminates – negatively discriminates – against women because they are not admitted to combat divisions, and "male culture" is sometimes applied in a derogatory way toward the military organisations. Implicit in this decrying is that there is no sex-specificity in identity and in action. I do not subscribe to this position, and, in our present cultural context, some things I say are contentious. In order to progress the discussion, it is necessary again to draw on the distinction between *sex* and *gender*.

Sex and Gender

When I was young, we hardly heard about "gender". We were taught that English was largely a "gender neutral" language, with a few exceptions such as a ship was "she" and the land Australia was "she" – that is, was feminine gender, not neutral gender. Nowadays we are asked our "gender" when "sex" is meant. I am a male not because of some linguistic or other cultural observance. I am a male because at conception a Y chromosome cell from my father joined with an X chromosome cell from my mother, resulting in a zygote of XY chromosomal structure, thereby determing my male sex. That cell from my father, *spermatozoon*, could have been X chromosome marked. In which case, joined with the maternal X chromosome, female sex is determined. That is, male *spermatozoa* ("semen" or "sperm") is about 50/50 Y or X, but the female *ovum* ("egg") is always X. Thus, it is the male parent who determines the sex at conception, and the normal human male at a cellular level is constructed on an XY pattern, while a normal human female at a cellular level is constructed on an XX pattern. When we fill out a Census form, we should be marking Male or Female as "sex", not as "gender".

Speaking of "manliness" or "womanliness" would be decried by those who approach such things as simply "cultural", or even "personal choice". Such persons may want that a man who has undergone hormone treatment and surgery and identifies as a woman should be able to state "Female". The fact remains that such changes are only cosmetic – only matters of appearance – and do not change the genetic fact of maleness. A fundamental fact of human nature is that we are permanently sexually differentiated as Male and Female. And a fundamental fact of that sexual differentiation is that the human male carries the chromosomal marking of both male and female, while the human female carries the chromosomal marking of her own sex only. We properly speak of "sex", and cannot displace it with a socially-constructed "gender".

Sexual identity

Nevertheless, there are complex processes that are both genetic, cultural, and personal in how sex is identified and is acted out. Our sexual identity is partly genetic, and is partly cultural and/or personal. A guy's personality and behaviour is hugely influenced by the fact that his hormonal production is mainly *testosterone*, while a gal's personality and behaviour is hugely influenced by the fact that her hormonal production is mainly *oestrogen*. Nevertheless, cultural and personal factors play a substantial role in psychological development and in the emergence of patterns of behaviour.

This can lead to variation in what is reckoned as "masculine" or as "feminine", or what is recognised as not being marked as "masculine" or "feminine" – that is, what is marked as somewhat "gender neutral". So, for example, wearing trousers may be marked as "masculine", or may be marked as "masculine" *or* "feminine". But even so in such instances, *sex* will usually be in evidence – for example, a gal's backside is usually going to look rather different in trousers than a guy's backside. But in some contexts, it may be regarded as "feminine" to wear trousers, and in some contexts some gals may choose to wear trousers whether it is thought fitting or otherwise. That is, some contexts read the cultural signals of masculinity and feminity differently; some contexts allow more flexibility in the expression of those signals; and some persons choose a more forthright manner in their choice of expression by giving less observance to common cultural signals. In brief, aspects of "gender" can be "culturally constructed" and/or "personally constructed".

Provided that "sex" and "gender" are not confused, I generally do not have a problem with that mobility – so long as the "mobility" observes something that is core;

namely, one's maleness or femaleness. That is, one can rightly speak of "manliness" and of "womanliness", and, indeed, one *should* speak of manliness and womanliness. To confuse them and/or to elide them works against respect for persons and psychological maturity. That said, it nevertheless is generally the case that maturity in manliness and womanliness is gained within a complementarity between the sexes, and not in isolation.

Sexual and gender complementarity

The most fundamental complementarity between men and women is that human male is designed to be a *father*, and human female is designed to be a *mother*, and that neither can be either without the other. Man and Woman are made for each other, and without their complementarity there is no parenting, and no children. This complementarity remains generally accepted in biological terms – except among those who want to define humanity through technological intervention (such through recourse to medical procurement of egg and sperm, contrived laboratory fertilisation, and contrived zygote implantation).

But psychology and biology are not simply distinct spheres. A woman experiences more physical restriction as pregnancy proceeds (it is not accident that birthing is called "confinement") and this calls upon the greater physical freedom, provisioning, and protection of the father. The mother lactates, and the father does not, and this integrates with the maternal nurturing role and reinforces the paternal provisioning and protecting role. The role and behavioural distinctions between the sexes are not adequately regarded simply as "cultural products":

in significant respects they are inherent. I remember years back an academic colleague (a rather "modern man") remarking after his third child and first daughter had left the cot, "We are not treating her differently; *she* is treating us differently!" The parents were discovering sexual differentiation in psychology and in behaviour as between their sons and their daughter that they could not attribute to different patterns of nurture.

An examination of one's own mental pictures (or else examining a photo file) shows this pattern under reinforcement. Daughters treat their father differently than do sons; the pattern by child age of child-father relations differs between daughters and sons. There is much social science research that is directed to showing how psychology and behaviour patterns by sex are *explained* by differences in culture and/or socialisation. It would be truer to interpret the evidence that culture and socialisation *reinforce* differences in psychology and behaviour, but do not "create" them (do not *explain* them). This reinforcement can be dysfunctional where it is highly stereotypical: that was part of my point in observing that the human male has both X *and* Y chromosomes, and that the human female *mainly* produces oestrogen hormones while the human male *mainly* produces testosterone hormones (with "mainly" conveying the sense of "not solely").

Complementarity does not necessarily involve exclusiveness, and there can be overlap in male attributes and behaviour and female attributes and behaviour. It remains true however that *sex* is, so to speak, the "departure point" for this overlap in complementarity, and that *gender* strongly relates to sex. In psychological terms, *sex* is the "leader" in the inter-psychic and intra-psychic construction of *gender identity*. And, further, this construction of differentiated gender identity (like the sexual differentiation) depends upon complementarity. "Masculineness" compares with "feminineness" (and "feminineness" compares with "masculineness") not as sharp polarities, but as overlapping complementarities. A mature *manliness* is worked out in relation to a mature *womanliness* (and mature womanliness in relation to mature manliness). The emergence of a healthy and mature gender psychology involves and evokes an inter-relatedness between the sexes.

Inter-relatedness between the sexes

One of the huge difficulties that we face with marriage in contemporary societies (that is, in "Western" contemporary societies) is a growing implicit denial of this differentiated complementarity. Man and woman "equal" seems to be taken as a mathematic statement, when it is not. And it is unfashionable to explicate this fact. A telling example is in the *Catechism of the Catholic Church*, where the differences in role and responsibility of the husband and wife are hardly treated. The only clear naming of which I am aware is in the Preface for the Eucharistic Prayer on the Solemnity of St Joseph, where Joseph is named as "... that just man, that wise and loyal servant, whom you [that is, God] placed at the head of your family ...".

Such language is contentious language for contemporary society. It is language to which I ascribe. A husband and father "heads" the household, not to oppress his wife and children, but for the good order of the family. As "head" a husband does not "lord it over" his wife, but he generally takes the lead and the protection of the family. This lead is, however, exercised in a spirit of partnership with his wife and with respect for his wife as sharing his human dignity. In the earlier chapter on immaturity among men, I initially was disposed to speak of "men behaving badly" as *unmanly*. The *manly* behaviour of a man is part of his masculinity and a manifestation of his manly maturity.

In a sense, manly identity is best exemplified in the man who is a husband. But the observation also applies to men who are not married. For example, the young man who has not gained a relational ease with young women is not mature in his manliness; and a priest whose pastoral aptitudes do not extend to women does not manifest a maturity in his manliness. I of course do not imply that everyone does or should achieve high relational mobility between the sexes. We sometimes hear the phrase "A man's man" to describe a man who gets along better with blokes, but where his manly maturity is not in question. The fact of my writing a book like this itself evidences that I have a better grasp of male psychology than female psychology, but it does not mean that I devalue a feminine psychology or lack appreciation of male and female inter-relatedness in the processes of psychological maturation.

The general pattern of pychological maturation involves the interplay between the masculine and the feminine. What I have reinforced with my example of St Joseph is that masculine identity and behaviour differ in important respects from feminine identity and behaviour. The earlier example of combat soldiers is another case in point. I have never heard a man who is or has been a professional soldier say or imply that he *liked killing*. Across decades of working with military men, I have never heard a professional soldier declaim that women should normally be admitted to the ranks of *killers* (in the professional warrior sense). These are but two and pointed examples of where an undue blurring of gender identity in contemporary society gives rise to confusion in sexual identity of a kind that fosters intra-psychic and inter-psychic dysfunction – confusion that detracts maturity in manliness and womanliness. This diminishes the dignity of men *and* of women, and in men leads to psychological profiles and behaviour that are *unmanly*.

Unmanliness toward women

There is a marvellous line in *Middleharch*, a brilliant psychological novel by a nineteenth-century woman who wrote under the name George Eliot, where the novelist says of Dr Lydgate, "He desired not a wife, but an ornament." That is, this gifted physician and scientist did not truly seek a partner in marriage, but a beautiful ornament who would enhance his professional and social standing. Eliot might instead have portrayed a man who wanted sex, or a man who wanted a house servant. There are any number of reasons why a man might want a wife, and a good one. A simple glance at the typical wedding photographic portraits shows brides looking somewhat "ornamental" on their husbands' arms, and there is nothing wrong with that; nor is there anything wrong with sex, and in fact it is integral to married life; nor is there anything wrong with a measure of task differentiation by sex, and this typically leads to more productive family lives.

But a woman is not simply ancillary to a man. A manly man does not look at life simply from *his* perspective and simply from *his* wants. Marriage is a partnership. A wife's beauty is different from a husband's beauty; a wife's sexual desires and performances have their own métier and are not simply her husband's; and wifely aptitudes and skills are not simply ancillary to her husband's and will have their own variety and make-up that need to be acknowledged and respected. Fulfilment is not simply a *husband's* project (nor simply a *wife's* project). For the married, fulfilment is a stable joint project for their mutual fulfilment, for the fulfilment of children as the fruit of their marriage, and for the good of society. A mature man has an ease in engaging women in his life's project.

This principle is well set forth in the example of marriage, but it has its own applicability in life generally. The principle now current of "equal opportunity" has much to commend it. I am always amazed when I see a huge delivery van reversed into a loading bay with such exact precision, and I expect I'd be surprised if the driver who jumped out were a woman. Men generally have enhanced skills in spatial judgement, and their "truck like" bodies fit with "truck like" work. But I would regard it as "discrimination" if guys cold-shouldered in that occupational line a woman who had the aptitudes for that work.

In education, in the workplace, and in so many social situations, we observe overlap and flexibility in aptitudes and skills profiles between men and women. A mature man is not phased by this, and does not hold back on respect for and co-operation with women in the variety of life situations. To do so would be *unmanly*.

These observations are of course generalisations, and generalisations have exceptions that are not "exceptional". It is not exceptional for guys only to play in a football team; they need to pit themselves against *guys*, and need to play with a "guy psychology" as well as a "guy physiology". Likewise, there is nothing exceptional in "men's shed" activites where guys just relax with other guys in a "guys only" environment where they talk about "guy things" and enact "guy things" such as car restoration, carpentry, or whatever. And gal's in their own ways also construct "gals only" associations and activities. It is not difficult to tell when "guys only" domains become unhealthy, as unhealthy behaviour is observed.

Occasionally, for example, one sees coverage of some incident after a football game where the team has procured a "girl" and all the "boys" had sex with her. Such a grotesque example shows not simply something that is immoral, but something that manifests a collapse in the construction of a healthy manly identity. Although such "boys" would probably be taken-aback by such a portrayal, this kind of behaviour is also homosexual – for sexual performance and exhibitionism of this kind is for the "the boys", and the "girl" is just a toy (just a "cunt") for the amusement and immature egotism of "the boys". But the example *does not* demonstrate that a "boys only" football club and a "boys only" event celebration in itself is "unmanly". Such an example manifests only that the culture of a particular club or a particular set of guys is unmanly.

One can notice such unmanliness in less extreme examples than the one just given. Perhaps the surest common signal is derogatory language about gals, where womanly dignity, intelligence, and aptitudes are not respected. Put simply, it's a matter of guys recognising that they are not the "complete man". The "complete man" is man in relation to woman, and woman in relation to man. The "completeness" of each sex involves a complementarity of the sexes that upholds the dignity and the genius of each.

Manliness and womanliness in maturity

The argument in this chapter on sexual and gender complementarity has particular force with respect to the life-cycle maturation of children. Children are generally going to know their maternity, but knowing their paternity generally turns on their being conceived in and nurtured in the stable mutuality of marriage. Children have a powerful instinct to know their parentage, and this is perhaps more notable in paternity, and perhaps even more so for boys. The classical Greek "novel" *The Odyssey* is essentially about a boy's separation from his mother and his search for his father as a search for his own identity. Even in the absence of his father, his mother's communication of reverence, love and longing for her husband gives something to which the boy clings in the drama of his search and his finding – finding both his father, and "finding himself".

The power and poignancy of parents in the unfolding and growth in self-identity of their children applies both to daughters and to sons. The power and poignancy of the sexual and gender differentiation and complementarity of the parents applies both to daughters and sons. And the application does not stop with entry into "adulthood" and "maturity". People whose parenting has been inadequate and/or disrupted have a much harder life transition that those blessed with happy parenting. Whether as guy or as gal, throughout our lives we carry our experiences of parenting, and, where these were deficient, we work across many years to make up that lack.

Where as guy or as gal we have been blessed with happy parenting, we enjoy across many years the blessings of that happy and fruitful sexual and gender complementarity. The psychological resources gained from the early and later experiences of happy and fruitful parental complementarity continues as a resource for our more fruitful and happy living – and, for guys, continues as a resource for continuing growth in *manly maturity*.

13
Psychological Dynamics: the Maturing Experience

No recipe for "success"

Manly maturity has been used throughout the book for a quality of masculine character to which guys should aspire. It is a "warm words" phrase that probably appeals to most guys. There is however a problem that so far has not been squarely addressed – namely, that such a quality of masculine character will not necessarily bring "success" or "popularity". What is being proposed in this book is not simply a *How to succeed in life* or a *How to be liked in life*. This is not a "populist" book. A pointed example of this fact may be taken from the Old Testament book Wisdom which may be read substituting "a guy of manly maturity" for "the virtuous man":

> Let us lie in wait for the virtuous man, since he annoys us and opposes our way of life ... Before us he stands as a reproof to our way of thinking ... His way of life is not like other men's, the paths he treads are unfamiliar.
>
> In his opinion we are counterfeit; he holds aloof from our doings ... Let us test him with cruelty ... and thus explore this gentleness of his and put his endurance to the proof. (Wisdom 2:12-19)

It is perhaps not surprising to find such a text in biblical wisdom literature, but it perhaps is surprising to find that the kind of insights there captured also find place in the literatures of social psychology, moral psychology, and the psychology of social exclusion. A pointed example given below is drawn from a book titled *Social Cognition* edited by Joseph Forgas in a chapter by Daniel Wegner and Robin Vallacher entitled, " Common-sense Psychology" where it reads:

> Given the benefits of self-control and self-management [in the person who has self-knowledge], it might seem that people would be eager and willing to scrutinise their implicit theories and to change them when ineffective, immoral or undesirable features are discovered. The widespread occurrence of self-defeating behaviour, faulty judgement, and downright nastiness, however, reminds us that people are often very reticent to question their values and assumptions, even when these features of implicit theory are demonstrably wrong.

The uncomfortable fact is that people – whether they be "ordinary people" or "scientists" – generally prefer to "look through" their theories, rather than to "look at" their theories (that is, to examine their theories). This is so whether the "theories" are implicit or explicit. It is so because to "look at" is to question, and to question may be challenging.

Where people want to live settled lives, they do not want to be challenged. For many people – perhaps for most people – there is greater preference for being "comfortable" than for being "dynamic". Many people, even most people, prefer situations and people who are unchallenging. Many social situations and organisational forms are geared to *reinforce* "the way we do things", rather than to *examine* "the way we do things".

Someone who has undergone a dynamic process of self-knowledge and has constructed a personal maturity – in guy-terms, *manly maturity* – may be identified as someone who "rocks the boat"; as someone who is not part of the "in group"; or as someone who is not a "company man". And processes that may be described as the psychology of social exclusion will be encountered by such a guy who in the words from the book Wisdom "holds aloof from our doings".

While it is true that *manly maturity* is not necessarily a recipe for *How to succeed* or *How to be liked*, nevertheless such a quality of masculine character does allow a guy to deal more constructively and dynamically in many life situations – whether it be generally relating well with women in personal, social, and professional settings; adapting to difficult social situations and difficult people in personal, social, and professional settings; leading changes for the better in personal, social, and professional settings. The point that is underscored in opening this chapter is simply that such "success" is not guaranteed. A guy of *manly maturity* is not necessarily going to be a "hit", not necessarily going to be popular or liked.

The kind of person who first wants to be a "hit" is unlikely to persevere in the task of constructing and enacting *manly maturity*. Such a guy is more likely to "play the game", to be the "Mister Nice Guy", or to be the upwardly aspiring "Company Man". The dynamics of the maturing experience operate differently, and call upon different motivations; different values; and different skills and character development.

Psychological dynamics of manly maturity

Personality and manly maturity. There is no

"personality" that links to "manly maturity". Different men have different personalities, and personal maturity may occur across the range of personality types, and is not linked to one or another personality profile. Of course, where preferences as manifest in personality types are at one extreme or another (such as strong preference for closure ("J")), it follows that there is less likelihood of change processes involved in psychological maturation. But it remains the case that across the range of personality types, personal maturation can be engaged – although the dynamics of the maturation process will differ in ways that reflect personality differences.

Personality development and manly maturity. As implied in the previous sub-section, different personalities will have different developmental paths. But, again, it is to be emphasised that personality development does not follow one path or another. One can generalise about the path of personality development for one personality type or another, but not about the developmental path in more general terms.

The generalisation by one personality type or another follows from different personality types having different aspects of strength and not-so-strong aspects, and where personality development involves building upon strength aspects in a personality type to build-up not-so-strong aspects. A lead example in the chapter on personality development is where guys who are strong on cognitive mental processes ("T") develop competencies in more inter-relational mental processes ("F").

Maturity understood as psychological development. As explained in the chapter on

Developmental Psychology, investigation of this area has tended to focus upon child and adolescent years, and upon developmental stages. In the present context where those addressed are adults or emerging adults, earlier developmental stages are not as relevant, and, further, a step-wise stages approach is not as relevant. The important points to take away are that weak developmental experience in earlier life eras can to some extent be remedied in later life eras.

The issue thus becomes less one of developmental capacity as such, and more one of the *activation* of psychological developmental capacity. The activation of psychological developmental capacity in important respects is an enculturation and educational endeavour – an awakening people to personal maturation and cultivating a culture of personal maturation.

Guys whose formative years and years of emerging adulthood have not called forth nor been conducive to personal maturation may yet have psychological capacity that can be activated by goal-oriented experiences that induce engagement in personal development in areas that were lacking.

It is evident, however, that "development" is not always "positive" and that "decay" – rather than "development" in a positive sense – can often be observed among those who do not engage a developmental path in life. Moving through life eras in a manly way involves recognition of and engagement with the on-going task of personal development.

The development task is never an *achieved* task, but always a *work-in-progress*. The "manly maturity" of a 40-year-old guy is not that of a 60-year-old guy, and during "mature" decades the challenge and the task in a wider understanding of psychological development remains to be engaged. One of the sayings that I recall from my youth was, *There's no fool like an old fool!* This captures a commonplace understanding that personal development is a continuing project, even into old age.

Maturing and psychological intelligence. Observations already made also apply to psychological intelligence. Certainly, in the metaphor earlier used, "firepower" is more or less a given endowment, but the way that one uses one's "firepower" is not. In much the same way that one's physical type and physical strength has an element of givenness about it that yet can be modified through exercise regimes and lifestyles – so, too, building-up patterns of thinking and working at building-up patterns of thinking give rise over time to more intelligent thinking. This is true across the range of "thinking", whether it be more cognitive processes or more affective processes. Whether this occurs or not depends upon intra-psychic processes and activity, but it is also much influenced by inter-psychic processes and activity. Intelligent company cultivates intelligence in oneself, while persistent exposure to unintelligent company retards psychological intelligence. The development of mental skills is both a personal project *and* a social project, and guys who want to engage development in psychological intelligence need to access social relations that support their personal maturation.

Social psychology and maturity. Psychological intelligence can be thought of in terms such as intelligence for mathematical skills or intelligence in interpreting affective behaviours. The former understanding of intelligence tends to focus on intra-psychic processes, while social psychology and maturity focuses more on inter-psychic processes. The key in inter-psychic processes is *communication*. The term "communication" probably takes more immediate meaning in the sense of conversation and of media communication (such as newspapers and electronic media), but has been treated in the chapter on Social Psychology under the name of *social representations*. This conveys a sense that speech is not simply denotative in meaning (what the words precisely say), but is also connotative in meaning (associations that words evoke, such as familiar/unfamiliar or friendly/unfriendly), and also the tone of communication (same words, but different meaning according to the intonation used). This naturally widens to an appreciation of facial expressions and body gestures ("body language"), so that "speech" is not simply words, nor "text" simply writing understood in linear terms.

The way a person dresses involves social communication; the way a person deports himself (herself) involves social communication (such as a strut, rather than a walk). The kind of house in which one lives and the kind of car one drives involves social communications – they are "text" that can be "read". The different kinds of buildings are also social communications – a utilitarian office building can usually be "read" as such, and a court house "read" as such, a war memorial "read" as such, and so forth. Indeed, a whole civic environment can be "read" as a social representation.

Such acts of "reading" and of communication involve maturation in intra-psychic skills. An immature person does not know how to adapt his speech according to a reading of the relevant social representations; nor how to adapt his dress and deportment; nor what is fitting for one context of built environment, but not fitting for another context of built environment.

Flexibility and adaptability of this kind is an aspect of *maturity*. And where this maturity coheres with masculine personality, then flexibility and adaptability of this kind is an aspect of *manly maturity*. The way a guy speaks is expressive of his masculinity (and I do not simply refer to lower voice pitch that is part of our recognition of a male voice, rather than a female voice); the way a guy dresses is expressive of his masculinity; the kinds of buildings that guys choose are expressive of their masculinity; the ways that guys relate with other guys and the ways that guys relate with women are expressive of their masculinity. What is mainly operative in these communications, in these *social representations*, involves inter-psychic processes – inter-psychic processes that are *developmental*.

This developmental aspect is captured in commonplace language such as one might hear in respect of a teenager, "He's mature for his age." People recognise varieties of maturity – such as according to age; according to era; according to culture; according to context (formal/ informal, and so forth).

People also especially also recognise maturity in gendered terms. Yes, we may say, "Such and such is a mature *person*", but often what we say will be sexed and gendered – such as "He's such a gentleman!" or "She's a real lady!" That is, the dynamics of social psychology and maturity are also sexed and gendered. There may be some mobility, even some ambiguity, in respect of sex and gender in some contexts and circumstances and among some people. But generally speaking, social representation "texts" will have a *gendered quality*. This quality may be unrefined or brash, and sometimes this will be "okay" (such as when being "blokesy" fits the social context). Generally, however, the gendered quality involves a social adeptness and differing degrees of refinement that in respect of guys communicates a *manly maturity*.

Psychology of emotional maturity. There of course is an overlap between social psychology and maturity and the psychology of affect and maturity. But affective maturity is not necessarily social, and often the "reading" of one's emotions may be an intra-psychic activity. But the era of popularisation of "affective maturity" – more often under the label of "emotional maturity" or "emotional intelligence" – mainly focuses on inter-psychic aspects of moods and emotions. That is, "emotional intelligence" mainly treats aptitudes and skills engaged in communications that more involve "affect" than "cognition" – although, of course, all communications involve both cognitive and affective aspects, and often in mobile combinations and complex overlays.

Where affect is more operative, the sex and gender differences are often more marked. Something as simple as listening to the shrieks of a crowd in distress usually identifies mainly female shrieks; just noticing a social situation where grief is present usually identifies female weeping. More generally, however, the psychology of affect and the expression of affect are not so stereotypical. Guys and gals differ considerably in expressions of affect, and there is overlay in affective expression across guys and gals.

This necessary recognition of overlay between guys and gals nevertheless does not gainsay the fact of sexing and gendering in affect, both in feeling and in expression and communication of affect. There are male patterns in affect and there are masculine patterns of affect and its expression. And people are able in gendered terms to recognise and to adjudge whether the affect is masculine in its maturity or masculine in its immaturity. There thus is also a *manly* affective maturity.

Like other aspects of manly maturity, affective manly maturity is a continuing project, and different life eras bring different maturation challenges. One aspect of the dynamics that should again be emphasised is the significance of complementarity in both the development and the exercise of manly maturity – complementarity between different personalities, yes, but – especially – complementarity between guys and gals. The vitality of manly maturity is more fully seen when complementing and relating with the vitality of womanly maturity – and this is perhaps markedly so in respect of affective maturity. Guys generally develop in affective manly maturity in a dynamic that engages the affective womanly maturity of gals (and gals generally develop in affective womanly maturity in a dynamic that engages the affective manly maturity of guys).

As with all varieties of maturation, *motivation* plays a vital role. It is easier to be immature than to be mature, and the motivation for affective manly maturity is essentially going to be a desire appropriately to adjudge and to respond to the affective and cognitive responses of others in ways that are helpful. This "helpfulness" may not always be smooth – for one's version of "helpfulness" is going to be coloured by one's version of what is good. The motivation for "good" is a powerful driver for the manly affective maturity project, but it does not ensure that others will affirm one's version of the "good" and its affective recognition and expression. This leads to the next difficult and dynamic issue of *manly moral maturity*.

Moral psychology and maturity. Moral maturity is perhaps the most difficult area, because it is one that often least provides "success", the one that often is the most arduous maturity to gain and to sustain, and the aspect of human maturity that most depends upon intra-psychic motivation. The key dynamic for the development of moral maturity is a drive for justice – and justice that is given implementation in life. The dynamic of the search for justice calls for perseverance in that search. It follows that moral maturity comes neither easily nor quickly.

Because the formulation of just judgements and the enacting of justice often require complex and integrated thinking, frameworks for cognitive processes also need to be built both intra-psychically and inter-psychically in order to bring adequate formulation and processing of the considerations entering the making and the enacting of just decisions.

Frameworks or schemata for the formulation, processing, and articulation of moral reasoning and action do not just "happen". These frameworks are gained by progressive activities of psychic construction, both intra-psychic and inter-psychic.

Particularly in their communication, moral reasoning and action calls upon what has already been rehearsed as social representations. This is a particularly difficult aspect, as it is often the case that the social representations are *not* shared. People may have quite different moral life schemata that give rise to quite profound conflict in matters of moral judgement and action. Often the different schemata will be implicit. And implicit schemata often will not have been worked through in an articulated manner, and their components and the congruence of their components (or the incongruence of their components) may be unexamined.

The frequent lack of examination makes for difficulty in calm consideration of differences in moral perspective and action. And this lack of commonality (including a lack of shared social representations) may make great calls upon emotional maturity, great calls upon temperance. Without emotional maturity, mature moral understanding may not issue in mature moral practice in relating with others who do not comprehend and/or do not agree with a scheme of moral reasoning and action. Moral maturity tends to complexity not only within its own domain, but also tends to complexity in its integration with other domains, such as those evoked by the terms "social representations" and "emotional intelligence".

When these complexities of maturation are considered,

their dynamics for guys calls upon recognition of differences between men in general and women in general in processing, decision, and action in moral domains. Men on the whole tend to more abstract cognitive reasoning in such matters, while women on the whole tend to relational reasoning that gives different weight to context (to social context). This means that the tendency of guys to focus on *content* reasoning often needs to be expanded more to include *context* reasoning (while the tendency of gals to focus on context reasoning often needs to be expanded more to include content reasoning). Lest the reader should begin to think that I am being sexist (despite my use of language that does not imply guys simply do *content* reasoning, or that gals simply do *context* reasoning), I urge that readers be mindful of the tendency both of guys and of gals to contaminate reasoning with *affect*.

Guys and affect contamination in moral reasonings. Where such affect contamination occurs (whether with guys or with gals), the reasoning process becomes driven by emotional foundations that often are taken as "given", and not examined. One can encounter quite complex reasoning that yet does not make sense because it depends upon some emotional attachment that is not part of the reasoning. It is a mark of moral maturity in some measure or another to detach reasoning processes from one's like and dislikes. But the capacity to reason calmly about something that evokes "like" or "dislike" (even strong "like" or "dislike") is a mark of moral maturity, and it is a mark that in psychological terms requires robustness that is built by over-time practice.

This brings us back to the base dynamic of the search

for justice, a search that may even be contrary to one's dispositions in terms of "likes" or "dislikes". Justice may serve the interests of the one who adjudges and acts justly, but it also may *not* serve the interests of the one who adjudges and acts justly. It may be costly. For many, it may be too costly.

Maturity is not simply psychological, because in the moral dimension it also takes us into *virtue*. Virtue involves not what one likes or dislikes, but what is just or unjust, what is good or bad. Psychology as a discipline does not hold sway in matters of virtue, and psychological maturity alone is not going necessarily to deliver virtue, and not going necessarily to deliver virtue such as marks *manly maturity*. It is courage and conviction that carry a guy through the enacting of *manly moral maturity*.

Immaturity among men: autocrats and cowards

Autoctrats. The dynamic of autocracy is personal insecurity that provokes a desire to control. Personal growth is closed off for autocrats, because they are people who manage others, rather than themselves. Maturity involves the development of self-management aptitudes and skills and the development of relational skills with others. In own-person terms, such development calls upon a degree of introspection and in other-person terms calls upon a degree of openness and trust. Insecure people prefer not to "look inside" and in looking at others prefer not openness and trust, but attitudes of scheming, manipulation, control and contempt.

This perception of autocrats means that the autocratic

personality needs to be identified early before it gets amplified and before he is able widely to enact the autocratic tendency. The early signs are a lack of respect for due process (a lack of respect for disinterested administration of justice), along with a lack of regard for people and for their sensitivities and their rights. Where such people are given command, their command does not take the character of the authority of lawfulness and of reason. Their command takes the arbitrary character of diktat and of concealment of means of control (whether this be such as the "secret police"; financial manipulations; or emotional oppression say of wife and children).

There thus is a great need for early recognition of the personality traits that are manifest in such behaviours, and – where possible – restricting the rise of such persons. In social situations this requires the institutionalisation of due process and of accountability as normal practice. Autocrats rise where social institutions are under stress, and where persons of differing interests or different interest groups do not find or are unable to find consensus. Autocracy flourishes in such situations of social instability (such as arise from unresolved class or ethnic conflicts) and in situations of personal instability (such as a cowardly wife).

Ironically, autocrats are usually also cowardly, and when caught-out tend to go into hiding or to take flight. But typically their cowardice is camourflaged with bravado – and bravado that is augmented by those who gather around the autocrat as a means of securing their own undeserved preferment. This is why the absence or weakness of social institutions that restrict autocracy (such as institutionalised transparency and accountability) mean that the "way forward" in the face of autocracy usually involves not transition, but displacement – often through revolution and warfare (whether of the "guns" variety or of "other" varieties).

Successful "warfare" is not governed simply by numbers, yet rarely will a solitary actor be able successfully to curb an autocrat. Typically, concerted social action of "guns" and/or "other" varieties will be necessary. From a psychological viewpoint, this involves a psychological reckoning of the conditions for effective social organisation to counter and/or to displace the autocrat, and psychological reckoning of the conditions for building a viable alternative social organisation. In brief, this involves bringing a psychological manner of thinking to political and organisational ways of thinking – a kind of "psychology of reform".

Cowardice. Cowardice takes many forms, and autocracy arises where cowardice is combined with the lust for power in answer to personal and social insecurity. Typically, we think of cowards as those whose disengagement from circumstances of conflict is fueled by a lack of desire for power. The bravado of the autocrat positions him (it is usually a "him") at the front of the crowd. What is more typically identified as cowardice positions him (or her) at the back of the crowd; or surrounded by cronies; or running away from the action; or seemingly just making oneself unnoticed in conflictual situations. Men of bravado do not necessarily have convictions and their "conviction" slogans on examination may be seen as no more than slogans.

The more identified coward is marked by lack of depth comprehension of justice issues. The coward does not really stand for anything. Cowards are simply weak personalities. They may seem harmless, but in situations of reform or change, they can be quite dangerous, because they will simply keep quiet when the "old guard" is quashing any reform or simply keep quiet when some abuse needs to be exposed. Again, early identification of the personality type is the best strategy, and then acting to ensure that whatever needs to be done does not depend upon their collaboration.

Immaturity among men: key sexual issues

Sometimes the dynamic in irresponsible sexual behaviour among men is simply the strength of the physical urge. As I elsewhere suggest (see end notes for the chapter), the delicate and difficult task of getting a rein on sexual instincts can be like training a stallion – and, without sustained patience in restraint, a guy's sexual instincts may become like a feral horse, like having a "brumby in a man's house".

The difficult task of restraint is much more possible where guys build a sense that they are not just "stallions", and that their sexual lives are more multi-dimensional than the phallus; and that sexual conduct integrates with the large project of constructing the capacity to enact moral conduct across a wide front of living.

Such a project integrates with an appreciation that coitus (at least for guys) is an inherently fertile act that potentially entails fatherhood. It is the potentiality of fatherhood that for guys particularly gives dignity to coitus – a dignity that entails its conduct in a relationship of stable commitment to the woman who may thereby become a mother, and a relationship commitment that is necessary to fulfilling child rights for fathering and mothering by parents stably known as "Dad" and "Mum" and as "husband" and "wife".

Constructing the requisite moral psychology for appreciating and enacting the sexual drives of a guy is an on-going task that requires courage and commitment. The guiding dynamic in this enactment is a mature conviction of the dignity and nobility of human sexuality, and its enormous power for joy and human good. Immaturity arises where the dignity, nobility, and goodness of male sexuality is undeveloped or under-developed.

An aspect of sexual immaturity that in the present era is inadequately identified as such is the enactment of homosexual behaviour (both male and female, but – in the present context – among guys). Acts involving anal eroticism are neither dignified and noble nor good. Moreover, they are acts that make recourse to human sensuousness of the era of pre-consciousness in erotic life. Making the identification of the sexual immaturity of such sexual enactments, and building psychological inhibitions against such sexual enactments is not the same as building inhibition of homosexuality as such.

In speaking of "homosexuality as such", the reference is not simply to same-sex attraction and same-sex interest. Everyone in one degree or another has same-sex attraction and same-sex interest: guys like competitive sport with guys and like elements of guys-only socialisation (as do gals). But this kind of same-sex attraction is not "homosexuality as such". Homosexuality occurs where the same-sex attraction is erotic and has a genital focus.

Yet I have not argued the building of psychological inhibitions against "homosexuality as such". The reason is that concerted inhibition of homosexual interest could lead only to suppression that is psychologically damaging. What I argue, rather, is the restraint – and in certain aspects, the inhibition – of the *enactment* of homosexual interest.

Where one has unrestrained and/or uninhibited enactment of homosexual attraction, one has the adoption of "gay" culture – the adoption of the attitude and the public display of the attitude that "the way I feel is the way I *am*; and that I am entitled to act out the way I am; it is my sexual right."

This is immaturity. The mature guy does not enact simply how he *feels*; he enacts according to what is good and what accords respect for the innate dignity and nobility of his human person and his sexual person, his *masculine* person, and the innate dignity and nobility of the person of the others with whom he enacts.

In maturity, all our enactments – whether heterosexual or homosexual – answer to this test of human nobility and the central and normative generative purpose of human sexuality. Our sexuality is not merely functional in its purposiveness, but neither is it simply "recreational". Human sexuality loses its dignity where it systemically is detached from its normally inherent fertility.

It is the reaching-out for fulfilment of purpose and for

manly nobility that is the chief motivation for engaging the project of manly maturity, including in its sexual aspect. We all long for fulfilment and for dignity. It is our searching enactments that provide the dynamic that brings what we long for – the fulfilment and dignity of *manly sexual maturity*.

Other issues

The dynamics of considerations treated in the chapter "Some Overview Perspectives" and in the chapter "Manliness and Womanliness in Maturity" are not rehearsed in this chapter. Some remarks are made on the dynamics treated in the chapter "Manly Mentoring for Maturity", and some further overall remarks on the dynamic nature of the maturation process, and applications using the rhetoric of goal-directed action.

Mentor listening. Perhaps the most crucial dynamic in mentoring for manly maturity is a clarity of respect for the mentoree, along with an acute *listening* to him. Young guys are more likely to open-up where the older guy implicitly conveys respect for them and for their capacity to build worthy lives, and where the older guy acutely listens to what they have to say.

Where the younger guy is quite young, he is more likely to say things that truthfully are but in the nature of explorations ("I would like to do such-and-such", or his the latest enthusiasm such as boxing or movies), and it is crucial that these enthusiasms not be put-down. Young guys need to be allowed to "dream dreams" (whether they be exalted dreams or pedestrian ones), and so to sort through what is going to be an on-going commitment for themselves, and to build themselves in readiness for later and more sturdy commitments.

An older guy acting as mentor can run before a younger guy some of the things that follow from one line or another of aspiration, and can lay before a younger guy things that need consideration in exploring, taking-up, or pursuing a certain line. But the advice – whether direct or covert – needs to maintain an it's-*your*-life attitude. A mentor cannot live the mentoree's life; it has to be *his* life. This is a crucial dynamic in any life era for the project of fostering *manly maturity*. Parents particularly need to be alert to this dynamic.

Mentor-enacted inspiration. After giving respect and a listening ear to the young, the biggest thing that a mentor can offer is inspiration – *enacted* inspiration. Young guys – like people in general – are more impressed when wisdom is *enacted*. It is the credibility of the older guy that is observed by the way that he conducts his life and that acts not simply as a "starter", but as a "driver" in a maturing mentor-mentoree relationship. The older guy has, in effect, to give a catechesis of virtues that is taught *by example*.

This manner of leadership should be of the kind that invites the younger guy to join on the journey, to join the challenge and adventure – and to do so as a *participant*. That does not mean the kind of "equalitarianism" that collapses differences of age, experience, and rank. But it means a genuine travelling together, adventuring together, that assists the younger guy to identify and articulate the way he is going and strengthens him in his choice – and strengthens also the older guy as he sees a younger guy take up the task of building a manly and a fulfilling life.

Mentoring "for a season". Sometimes this adventuring can be enduring: I have seen some of the young guys I have mentored build great personal, family, and professional lives and across decades maintain the mentoring relationship even as fully mature men. More often, the adventuring may be for a season or two, with the younger guy moving on with benefit from the mentoring relationship, but without sustaining the relationship.

The kind of grip that a mentor offers has to be of a firm manly kind, but not of a clinging kind: the love that a mentor offers has to be of the kind that leaves the younger guy free to move-on in a move-away sense. This is simply part of a dynamic that respects his person and his freedom, and that reflects a trust that in later years he will be generous with young guys and repay with manly love what he received as a younger guy.

Battle-scarred warriors. One of the character traits that younger guys look for in older guys is what I call "battle experience". An older guy has to be a man who knows about hard times, who knows about warfare, and who has some "battle scars", and who has come through "winning".

This particularly applies where younger guys are making choices that expose them to ostracism – to the effects of others practising various enactments of the psychology of exclusion.

Maturity is usually wrought in adversity, and mature men can flourish in adversity – they "come through" adversity winning, not necessarily gloriously and not necessarily with worldly acclaim, but nevertheless come through winning. It is communication of an attitude that pushes through adversity that will inspire a young guy and empower him to grow in manly stature so that he too comes through strengthened and equipped for life's challenges.

Many people live their lives as though in a "sleep" program, rather than an "awake" program, and live unalert lives. Many guys go through life as an "armchair exercise", and do not develop aerobic strength to run the distance, or anaerobic strength to push heavy weights. But mature manliness requires a wakeful alertness, and ability too endure, and an ability to press heavy weights – perhaps not literally in a gymnastic sense, but certainly literally in a realistic sense of developing manly character that is strong and virtuous.

"Develop it, or lose it!" Where this life challenge is not undertaken, the effects are atrophy. In just the same manner as muscles that are not used atrophy, and a body that is not used does not develop in manly strength, dexterity and muscularity – so too is it with manly character. So, too, is it with the mental aspect of manly character – an intelligence that is not used, not exercised, not methodically developed is an intelligence that will atrophy. It's pretty much a "use it or lose it!" The whole project of human development is a *dynamic* project and a project that *takes time*. The maturity project is on-going in its dynamism, and is never a "completed task". There always remains – in one degree or another – new maturings to be engaged, as manliness befitting different life eras is built.

This building is best understood in psychological terms, both intra-psychic and inter-psychic. It is a major life project for both guys and gals, but for guys it has a distinct masculine character that is both sexed and gendered. The approach adopted in this book necessarily focuses on what guys do in this project – on *what we do*. The closing chapter expands this perspective in respect of *what we do not do*. The *what we do not do* nevertheless involves our collaboration, our doing *what we do*.

14
Integrating Insights: a final word
What We Do Not Do

Having traversed a wide canvas of psychological approaches to *Manly Maturity*, I wish now to say that in certain respects what has been argued is radically incomplete. This is so because the book has focused on what *we do* – upon the intra-psychic and inter-psychic building or construction that we undertake, or – in *im*maturity – fail to undertake. The "incompleteness" is in the lack of attention to *what we do not "do"*. This "what we do *not do*" is *gift*, and is *God's gift*.

In terms treated in this book, we can identify "God's gift" in the aptitudes with which we are endowed and the strength that we receive to enact the psychic building of maturity. But acknowledging psychic endowment and psychic strength does not dispense the "incompleteness" of which I speak. To "complete" our understanding of the maturation process, we need an acute appreciation of the sublime nobility that God has given us and gives us in our creation. To this must be added an acute appreciation of the sublime nobility that God has given us and gives in *re*-creation.

This sense of "re-creation" crucially turns on a sense of *sin*, upon a sense of the need to "*re*-make". This re-making or re-creation requires an action that only God can supply (an action that we cannot "do"). This "action" upon us and in us is an undeserved generosity of God that is properly termed *grace*. And grace comes to us from a re-creative act of God that is properly termed *salvation* and/or *reconciliation*. Necessarily it must be expected that I should locate this act of re-creation in the person of Jesus of Nazareth, *the Christ*. So to confess is an *act of faith*. To engage this act of faith requires a gift of the same name, *faith*. Without *faith, Manly Maturity* and the whole maturation process and experience becomes simply a human work, becomes simply something that we "do".

There is, indeed, much that we can "do", and this book has outlined this on a wide canvas. I nevertheless hold the deepest conviction that this "doing" must engage a sense of *gift* and be enacted calling upon *grace*. This keen sense of giftedness from God and grace from God itself builds upon an *act of faith*, with the presupposition of faith and the living of faith also being understood as a gift, the gift of *faith*.

In the language here used, *faith* might well be thought of as something cognitive – whether intra-psychic or inter-psychic. Such a cognitive approach more nearly captures what is meant by "the faith" – meaning the doctrinal content that is appropriated in personal or intra-psychic acts and/or the doctrinal content that is appropriated in social or inter-psychic acts of the faith community. This is what is termed "the faith of the Church" or simply "the Faith". These senses are important and fundamental, but they do not capture what is fundamental in the simple term *faith*.

I say this because *faith* is not simply something "cognitive", whether cognitive in an intellectual sense or in an affective sense. Yes, faith takes cognitive form, including affective cognitive form. But psychological understandings do not quite comprehend *faith*. It might seem a "cop out" to say "Faith is a mystery". But the fact is that faith *is a mystery*. At least, I have found faith to be a mystery. In psychological terms I do not quite understand why I have *faith*, but I know that I *have* faith. I do not understand how some people have faith, and some people do not have faith. I understand something of how faith is increased, and I understand something of how faith is decreased or even lost. In saying "I understand something", I mean to convey that my understanding gives some measure of insight only, and that a sense of mystery remains.

Where a "sense of mystery" does not prevail, I am able to speak about "what *I do*" or "what *we do*", and when I cast this speaking in intra-psychic and/or inter-psychic terms, I convey psychological understanding. Where this psychological understanding nevertheless proceeds with a sense of "what *God is doing*", it proceeds with a sense of *grace*. This sense of grace has been in the background throughout this book. But it is fundamental to the thesis of this book. My conviction is that without grace, either "maturity" is not advanced or is defectively advanced. Without *grace*, we deal with what "*I* do" and/or what "*we* do" and do not engage what "*God* does".

From the perspective of "where I come from", a simply "humanistic" understanding of "maturation" and "maturity" gives rise to certain psychological competencies, but to competencies that tend to an arrogance and self-assertiveness. It gives rise to a "maturity" that lacks *kindness* and that lacks *humility*.

Such a "maturity" is *un*-gracious, and is not the *maturity* espoused in this book.

I am thus brought to the point where I may make explicit the source of the book title, *Manly Maturity*. It derives from a phrase in chapter 4 and verse 13 of the Letter of the Apostle Paul to the Church at Ephesus, commonly referred to as *Ephesians*. In this he speaks of equipping those who have faith in Christ to "… attain … to mature manhood, to the measure of the stature of the fulness of Christ …." In the usual language of the New Testament, humanity is typically referred to in the generic, *anthrōpos* / *anthrōpoi*, "man" in the generic or "humanity". In this text, St Paul uses the language of a male of our race, *andros*. I do not need here to explain why this language usage, and I certainly hold that both man, *andros*, and woman, *gunē*, are called to "fulness in Christ". But I am writing in a somewhat "feminist" era in which I find a diminution of masculine virtue. St Paul's text thus inspired the male and masculine focus of this book and the title *Manly Maturity*.

It would require another and a different book to expound *Manly Maturity* in theological terms and in spirituality terms. That is not something I have tried to supply. I have largely confined myself to what I advertise in the book sub-title – "psychological approaches to personal maturation". But it is essential that I should close this book making explicit that I see the maturation process and maturity in a context of *grace*. I see "manly maturity" as "*my* work" and "*our* work" and as "*God's* work in us". I do not see it as one *or* the other, as simply "humanistic" or as simply "God acting over and above us". My essential perspective is "incarnational", as captured and expounded in the Prologue of the Gospel according to St John: *And the Word became flesh.*

The great mystery of the gift of the Holy Spirit and the great mystery of the operations of the Holy Spirit find wonderful exposition in human maturity that is *gracious*. It is this gracious maturity that is alluded to in the book title *Manly Maturity*, and that is the background to the *psychological approaches* traversed in this book.

Chapter Notes

Chapter 1   Psychology and Personality

The opening paragraphs of this chapter draw on expressions found in the Preface of 1986 book by Albert Bandura, *Social Psychology of Thought and Action: a social cognitive theory* (Prentic Hall: Englewood Cliffs NJ). They were added late, and are congruent with what I have written throughtout the book.

There are many approaches to personality. The dominant one presented in this chapter is the schema developed by two American women, a mother and daughter, Katharine Briggs and Isabel Briggs Myers, typically referred to as Myers Briggs. The 1988 book *Type Talk* by Otto Kroeger and Janet M. Thuesen (Dell: New York) nicely captures the Myers Briggs schemata as used in my book. The survey data are drawn from a 1999 MBTI Manual, *A Guide to the Development and Use of the Myers-Briggs Type Indicator* by Isabel Briggs Myers et al (Consulting Psychologists Press and Australian Council for Educational Research: Melbourne). Myers Briggs typology is really a schematisation of the typological approach to personality expounded in a 1933 book by Carl Jung, *Psychological Types* (Harcourt, Brace and World: New York).

The recognition of the value of self-limitation in the adopting certain perspectives is drawn in its articulation from the closing chapter of a 1997 book by David C. Funder, *The Personality Puzzle* (Norton: New York), and again is congruent with what I had already written in my book.

Chapter 2   Personality Development

This chapter mainly present original perspectives, but ones informed by some key early psychologists, including Sigmund Freud who wrote in German and his 1940 book, *Abiss der Psychoanalyse* that was translated by James Strachley and published in 1949 as *An Outline of Psycho-Analysis* (Hogarth: London).

Chapter 3   Developmental Psychology

This chapter includes ideas drawn from Jean Piaget who wrote in French, and in the area here treated his contributions may be found in *La Psychologie de L'Intelligence*, published in 1947 and translated by Malcom Piercy and published in 1950 as Jean Piaget, *The Psychology of Intelligence* (Routledge & Kegan Paul: London). Summaries of the Piagetian approach may be found in most Psychology textbooks.

Chapter 4   Psychological Intelligence

I have been careful not to plagiarise in this book. Certainly I have been influenced by my reading, some of it over decades, but only occasionally have I closely followed some given author. In the area of intelligence testing, I have drawn on Anne Anastasi and Susana Urbina (1997), *Psychological Testing* (7e) (Prentice Hall: New Jersey). My account of basic IQ testing draws on their chapter 3. Their chapter 11 on the nature of psychological intelligence also informed my discussion, and also their chapter 13 on psychological issues in ability testing. My appreciation that intelligence is dynamic was reinforced in reading Anastasi and Urbina, and also reading a chapter by Robert J. Stenberg reinforced my appreciation of "successful intelligence" that underlies my basic approach (chapter 9 in James C. Kaufman (Ed.) (2009), *Intelligence Testing: integrating psychological theory and clinical practice* (Cambridge: Cambridge, UK)).

Chapter 5   Social Psychology and Maturity

Although this chapter is integrative in its insights, it has been much influenced by Joseph P. Forgas (Ed.) (1981), *Social Cognition: Perspectives on Everyday Understanding* (Academic Press: London), especially chapter 1, Forgas, J., "What is Social about Social Cognition?", pp. 1-26; chapter 7, Forgas, J., "Affective and Emotional Influences on Episode Representations", pp. 165-209; chapter 8, Moscovici, S., "On

Social Representation", pp. 186-210; chapter 9, Harré, R., "Rituals, Rhetoric and Social Cognitions", pp. 211-224; and chapter 12, Forgas, J., "Epilogue: Everyday Understanding Social Cognition", pp. 258-272.

Chapter 6   Psychology of Emotional Maturity

This chapter is integrative in its insights, although there are portions within this chapter that draw strongly upon Joseph P. Forgas and Carrie L. Wyland (2006), "Affective Intelligence: Understanding the Role of Affect in Everyday Social Behaviour", in Ciarrochi, J. et al (2006), *Emotional Intelligence in Everyday Life* (Psychology Press: New York), pp. 77-99.

Chapter 7   Moral Psychology and Maturity

Some important sources for the writing of this chapter are:

Albert Bandura (1986), *Social Foundations of Thought and Action: a social cognitive theory* (Prentice-Hall: Englewood Cliffs NJ).

Albert Bandura (1991), "Social cognitive theory of moral thought and action", in, Kurtines, William M. and Gewirtz, Jacob L. (Eds), *Handbook of Moral Behavior and Development: Volume 1: Theory* (Lawrence Erlbaum: Hillsdale NJ), pp. 45-103.

Lawrence Kohlberg (1976), "Moral states and moralization", in Lickona, T. (Ed.) *Moral Development and Behaviour* (Holt, Rinehart and Winston: New York).

William M. Kurtines and Jacob L. Gewirtz (1984), *Morality, Moral Behavior, and Moral Development* (Wiley: New York).

John Rawls (1971), *A Theory of Justice* (Harvard University Press: Cambridge, MA).

Manly Maturity has not been written as an academic book, and so citations do not appear within chapters. In most cases, where relying on other authors, I use ideas, rather than direct textual use. Bandura (1991) is an exception, and this chapter at points draws substantially on his treatment in this excellent and long article. At times this use has involved sentence modification that in academic works is identified by the use of three periods (…) or of square brackets [ ]. Such apparatus has not been employed where I have modified his text to fit my context, and I take this opportunity strongly to make acknowledgement of the contribution of Bandura (1991) is casting the chapter on Moral Psychology.

My own article, McGavin, P. A. (2011), "The Catechism on Sexuality: interpreting the "'constant tradition'", *Australasian Catholic Record*, 88(2): 219-231, extensively treats how moral reasoning that is tight syllogistically may yet be incomplete in a wider and contextualised evaluation.

Chapter 8   Immaturity among Men: wider-ranging issues

The treatment of power-centred men in this chapter has been influenced by the very large study by T. A. Adorno et al (1950), *The Authoritarian Personality* (Harper & Row: New York), and especially by the contribution of Else Frenkel-Brunswick in chapter 13, "Comprehensive Scores and Summary of Interview Results". This study attracted searching critique as in the also large volume edited by Richard Christie and Marie Johoda (1954), *Studies in the Scope and Method of "The Authoritarian Personality": Continuities in Social Research* (Free Press: Glencoe), and this extensive and complex critique sharpened my reading of Adorno et al (1950). A further critique by David W McKinney (1973), *The Authoritarian Personality Studies: an enquiry into the failure of social research to produce demonstrable knowledge* (Moulton: The Hague), provided yet further refinement. The sub-title of this second critique in a sense captures the protest following *The Authoritiarian Personality*. The protest arose in a context where the then dominant paradigm for the discipline of Psychology was "behaviouralism", and the methods pursued by Adorno et al were not simply "behaviouralist", and their hypothesis formulation and extensive and complex statistical work were not above criticism. Further, the approach to personality – not least in Frenkel-Brunswik – somewhat focused on early-life experience in the formation of personality from a Freudian perspective. This focus contributed to the "dark" personality assessment in their study and was contrary to the then contemporaneous ascendancy of "behaviouralism". This resulted in generally unfavourable professional assessment of the Adomo et. al. (1950), where the personality of the power-centred parson is seen as the main determinant of behaviour. Psychology as a discipline – while not shedding "behaviouralism" – has since the 1980s become less wedded to the behaviouralist paradigm, and so the critique of *The Authoritarian Personality* may not now be as severe. For myself, I still find this 1950 book a landmark study, and am not troubled by a measure of adherence to its central thesis, depiction, and conclusions on "the authoritarian personality".

The section in this chapter that treats the psychological processes of the cultivation of deceit draws upon the Bandura, "Social congnitive theory of moral thought and action", cited in the earlier chapter on Moral Psychology. Observations on social exclusion were sharpened by my reading a 2005 book, Kipling D. Williams et al (Eds), *The Social Outcast: ostracism, social exclusion, rejection, and bullying* (Psychology Press: New York). Much material in this chapter, like much of the book generally, draws on pactictical experience over many decades and diffuse relevant reading.

Chapter 9   Immaturity among Men: key sexual issues

Notes to chapter in this book are mainly addressed, not to guiding readers' further reading, but to ensuring adequate citation of sources and avoiding what might be construed as plariarism. This chapter reflects reading, thought, and

clinical experience across decades. The only references that
need citation are Sigmund Freud on the pervasiveness of
underlying sexual perversions and the psychological processes
that inhibit their being acted-out; and Freud's appreciation of
unhibited resort to infantile auto-erotic sensuality as *regressive*
behaviour. These insights were heightened in reading Freud's
early 1900s essays replublished in 1991 as Sigmund Freud,
Three Essays on the Theory of Sexuality and Other Works
(Penguin: London), and his 1940 book cited in the notes to
Chapter 3, above. A 2012 paper of mine that gives practical
consideration to equable treatment in particular cases of male
homosexual orientation is, McGavin, P. A. (2012), "A closer
look at discernment on homosexuality and the priesthood",
Australasian Catholic Record, 88(1):63-68. Some wider issues
in male psycho-sexual maturation are treated in, McGavin, P.
A. (2011), "Celibacy and Male Psycho-Sexual Development",
Journal of Pastoral Care & Counseling, 65(4):2:1-11.

Chapter 10 Manly Maturity:
Overview Perspectives

No specific references are cited for this chapter.

Chapter 11 Manly Mentoring for Maturity

The approach to mentoring for maturity presented in this chapter
largely arises from practical experience and engagement with
young men across several decades. Some have been notably
significant in forming these ideas and in the inspiration that
comes from relating with emerging adults. None, however,
should be singularly noticed – for the experiences have more
been collaborative than individual; and none should have the
positions presented in this book attributed to them, rather than
to the author alone. A book that was useful in sharpening the
articulation in this chapter (but not in introducing ideas new
to my experience) is *Emerging Adults in America: coming of
age in the 21ˢᵗ century* edited by Jeffrey J. Arnett and Jennifer

L. Tanner – particularly chapters by the Editors. Some further observations on the approach presented in this Mentoring chapter occur at in the notes for Chapter 13 on Psychological Dynamics.

Chapter 12 Manliness and Womanliness in Maturity

This chapter is one where I first hestitated in writing, as a man who has never engaged in erotic or romantic relationship. I found courage in reflection that across decades I have however had extensive relationships with women as well as men and that my understandings and my identity have been greatly influenced by many and extended professional and friendship relations with women. I thus at a late writing stage and while in Rome "took up the pen" and wrote this important chapter in portraying manly maturity. No specific references are cited.

Chapter 13 Psychological Dynamics: the maturing experience

Since this chapter mostly gathers earlier chapters, there is no need to repeat sources, but the long quote on the second page of this chapter shows the influence of the chapter, "Common-sense psychology" by Daniel M. Wegner and Robin R. Vallacher from the 1981 book *Social Cognition: perspectives on everyday understanding* edited by Joseph P. Forgas (Academic Press: London), and the expressions of "looking through" rather than "looking at" theories is also drawn from that chapter.

I spoke in the chapter about "as I elsewhere suggest" with reference to the difficult topic of manly maturation in its sexual aspect. The allusion is to learned journal articles of mine: "The Catechism on Sexuality: interpreting the 'constant tradition'" published in 2011 in *The Australasian Catholic Record*, 88(2):219-231, and "Celibacy and Male Psycho-Sexual Development" also published in 2011 in *Journal of Pastoral Care & Counseling*, 65(4): 2-1-11.

The articulation of ideas on mentoring include ones earlier mentioned from *Emerging Adults in America: coming of age in the 21ˢᵗ century* edited by Jeffrey J. Arnett and Jennifer L. Tanner. But I have added some reference to "goal-directed action". The phrase is taken from the title of a 1982 book edited by Mario von Cranach et al, *Goal-Directed Action* (Academic Press, London), but I have not made use of the book itself because I am not drawn to its positivist methodology. A more useful methodological paradigm for this kind of learning is that now called "action research", where the "subjects" of the learning/research process themselves become engaged in the learning/research process, and the learning and the maturation project becomes *co-operative*. A more rigorous expositon of this approach than has been applied in this book is well set forth in a 2007 book, *Action Research* by Ernest T. Stringer (Sage: London).

Chapter 14 Integrating Insights: a final word What We Do Not Do

There are no specific acknowledgements to be made in respect of this closing chapter – and at least except for Sacred Scripture, no *literary* acknowledgements. I have decided not to name the many persons who across what is now becoming a long life who have accompanied me on the journey toward maturity. I am immensely indebted to them, but the list is long, and, moreover, I do not want anything that I write attributed to anyone but me – so they have my gratitude and the enfolding in a life of prayer with thanksgiving, but remain un-named. There are as many people – probably more people – who have *not* been companions in the usual sense, but who have been causes of grief. But they also have contributed to the reflections that are gathered with the literary sources acknowledged for earlier chapters; they, too, in different ways have contributed to the "action research" that is condensed in this book. Encountering immature and mean and thoughtless people – as we all do! – presents many opportunities for "flourishing in adversity"; and I am grateful that I have in several respects at least been able to flourish. And my hope is that this book will assist reflective readers also so to flourish in the unavoidable adversities of life and that the book will contribute to the experience of *joy* that is an integral part of life and of *manly maturity*.